Beginning Excel What-If Data Analysis Tools

Getting Started with Goal Seek, Data Tables, Scenarios, and Solver

Paul Cornell

Apress®

Beginning Excel What-If Data Analysis Tools: Getting Started with Goal Seek, Data Tables, Scenarios, and Solver

Copyright © 2006 by Paul Cornell

ISBN (pbk): 1-59059-591-2

Printed and bound in the United States of America 9 8 7 6 5 4 3 2 1

Trademarked names may appear in this book. Rather than use a trademark symbol with every occurrence of a trademarked name, we use the names only in an editorial fashion and to the benefit of the trademark owner, with no intention of infringement of the trademark.

Lead Editor: Jim Sumser
Technical Reviewer: Andy Pope
Editorial Board: Steve Anglin, Dan Appleman, Ewan Buckingham, Gary Cornell, Tony Davis, Jason Gilmore, Jonathan Hassell, Chris Mills, Dominic Shakeshaft, Jim Sumser
Project Manager: Beth Christmas
Copy Edit Manager: Nicole LeClerc
Copy Editor: Marilyn Smith
Assistant Production Director: Kari Brooks-Copony
Compositor: Linda Weidemann
Proofreader: Linda Seifert
Production Editing Assistant: Kelly Gunther
Indexer: Valerie Perry
Cover Designer: Kurt Krames
Manufacturing Director: Tom Debolski

Distributed to the book trade worldwide by Springer-Verlag New York, Inc., 233 Spring Street, 6th Floor, New York, NY 10013. Phone 1-800-SPRINGER, fax 201-348-4505, e-mail orders-ny@springer-sbm.com, or visit http://www.springeronline.com.

For information on translations, please contact Apress directly at 2560 Ninth Street, Suite 219, Berkeley, CA 94710. Phone 510-549-5930, fax 510-549-5939, e-mail info@apress.com, or visit http://www.apress.com.

The source code for this book is available to readers at http://www.apress.com in the Source Code section.

Contents at a Glance

Contents

Preface

When folks ask me what I do for a professional career, I usually tell them, "I write books about computers." For those who are computer literate, the discussion usually continues this way:

Them: "What subjects have you written about?"

Me: "Mostly about using Microsoft Excel."

Them: "Like using Excel to do what?"

Me: "Analyze data. In fact, I'm currently working on a book that will cover analyzing data using the Excel what-if tools."

Them: "What-if tools?' What are those?"

Me: "Goal Seek, data tables, scenarios, and Solver."

Them: "Hmm . . . I've never heard of those. What are they?"

At this point, because I really enjoy teaching people, it's very tempting to jump into computer-instructor mode and bend someone's ear for ten minutes about the Excel what-if tools. However, I know better than to do that. I've learned that the best way to explain these types of things to others is to first start by describing what kinds of problems that they were designed to address. Using this approach, here's a simple, brief way to describe the Excel what-if tools:

- You use Goal Seek in Excel when you want to work backward from a solution to a problem—when you know the result of a single worksheet formula but not the input value that the formula needs to figure out the result. For instance, Goal Seek would be a good way to get a rough estimate of how much you could afford to pay for a home mortgage if you already know the mortgage's interest rate, the mortgage term, and how much you were willing to pay on the mortgage each month.

- Data tables are helpful when you want to view and compare the results of all of the different variations of a formula on a worksheet. A simple example of this might be one of those multiplication tables or metric conversion tables that you learned in school.

- Scenarios are a great tool for saving, in a worksheet, sets of values that Excel can switch between automatically so that you view different results. For instance, you could create best-case and worst-case scenarios, and then compare these scenarios' results next to each other.

- You use Solver when you want to work backward from a solution to a problem. It's similar to Goal Seek, but you use Solver when you also want to apply restrictions on the problem. Using the previous Goal Seek example, you could use Solver if you wanted to further restrict the total home price to not exceed a certain price.

This book is packed full of tutorials and exercises to help you learn about and master the Excel what-if tools at your own pace. My hope is that you will use this book first as a tutorial to learn about the tools, and then come back to it often as you need further help or simply a technical refresher.

I hope you enjoy reading and using this book as much as I enjoyed writing it.

Best wishes,
Paul Cornell

About the Author

For the past six years, **PAUL CORNELL** has been involved in creating documentation for Microsoft Office System business solution developers. Paul has contributed to developer documentation for Microsoft Office VBA Language References, Microsoft Office Primary Interop Assemblies, Microsoft Office Web Services Toolkits, and other Office development technologies. Paul has worked as a web site editor and frequent web columnist for the Office Developer Center on the Microsoft Developer Network (MSDN). Paul is currently the Documentation Manager for Microsoft Visual Studio Tools for the Microsoft Office System and the Microsoft Visual Studio core integrated development environment (IDE). Paul lives in the mountains of Washington with his wife and two daughters.

About the Technical Reviewer

ANDY POPE is a computer programmer living in Essex, England. He has been awarded the title Excel MVP by Microsoft each year since 2004. As well as being an active member of several web-based Excel forums and newsgroups, Andy maintains a web site focusing on Excel charting, at `http://www.andypope.info`.

Andy's active involvement within the online Excel community would not be possible without the support and understanding of his partner Jackie and especially their two children, Hannah and Joshua.

Acknowledgments

I want to give my deepest thanks to my wife, Shelley, for her constant love, encouragement, support, and counsel as I wrote this book. Without her, there's no way I could have put this book into your hands.

I also want to thank my two extra-special daughters for giving up a lot of their playtime with me while I worked on this book.

Thanks also to the staff at Apress for the opportunity to write this book, including: Gary Cornell, Apress Founder; Dominic Shakeshaft, Editorial Director; Jim Sumser, Lead Editor; Beth Christmas, Project Manager; Marilyn Smith, Copy Editor; and Andy Pope, Technical Reviewer. Also thanks to Kari Brooks-Copony, Beckie Stones, and Tina Nielsen at Apress for their help.

I want to thank my parents, Paul and Darlean, for their continued support and encouragement.

Finally, I want to thank God for helping me acquire the knowledge and skills I needed in order to write this book.

Introduction

Consider the following two story problems:

If I ride a bicycle 5 miles in 20 minutes, how long would it take me at that speed to ride my bicycle 20 miles? At that speed, how far could I ride my bicycle in 45 minutes?

If I earn $25.00 per non-overtime hour at a job and I work 45 hours per week, how many weeks would I need to work to earn $30,000 before taxes? How much would I earn before taxes if I worked a 50-week work year and took the remaining two weeks off without pay?

Here are the answers to these story problems:

It would take me 80 minutes to ride my bicycle 20 miles if I were riding it 5 miles in 20 minutes (that is, 15 miles per hour). At that speed, in 45 minutes I would ride my bicycle 11.25 miles.

I would need to work between 25 and 26 weeks to earn $30,000 if I earn $25.00 per hour working 45 hours per week (assuming I am paid one-and-one-half times my hourly rate for all hours worked over 40 per week). At that pace, I would earn $59,375 if I worked 50 weeks that year and took the remaining two weeks off without pay.

These are a few simple examples of the types of problems that the Microsoft Office Excel what-if data analysis tools are designed to solve quickly. This book teaches you how to use these tools.

In short, *what-if analysis* is the process of changing the values in certain worksheet cells to see how those changes affect other worksheet cells. For example, you could try varying interest rates for a home mortgage to determine the mortgage payment that you could afford to pay over a 15-year or 30-year mortgage term.

What Are the Excel What-If Data Analysis Tools?

The Excel what-if analysis tools include the following:

Goal Seek: When you know the desired result of a single formula that you want to achieve, but you do not know the input value that the formula needs to determine the desired result, you can use the Excel Goal Seek feature. Excel goal seeks by varying the value in a single worksheet cell until the formula that depends on that cell displays the desired result. For example, using the earlier bicycle example, at 15 miles an hour, you can adjust the number of minutes to 45 to determine how many miles you would travel at that rate (11.25 miles). In this case, the number of minutes is expressed as a formula (number of miles multiplied by the result of dividing 60 minutes by the number of miles per hour). The miles per hour are constant, and Excel is goal seeking to determine the number of miles traveled.

Data tables: A data table is a collection of cells that display how changing certain values in worksheet formulas affects the result of those applied formulas. Data tables provide a shortcut for calculating multiple versions in one operation, and a way to view and compare the results of all of the different variations together on your worksheet. Using the bicycle example again, you could create a table that summarizes the number of miles traveled at different speeds and different elapsed minutes traveled.

Scenarios: Excel can save a set of values and substitute them automatically in a worksheet to allow you to forecast the outcome of a worksheet model. You can create and save different scenarios on a worksheet, and then switch to any of these scenarios to view different results. For the bicycle example, you could switch between two or more different number of miles traveled using combinations of different speeds and elapsed minutes traveled.

Solver: Using Solver, you can find an optimal value for a formula in a target worksheet cell. Solver works with a group of cells related to a target cell's formula. Solver changes the values of adjustable cells to produce the desired result you specify in the target cell formula. You can also apply upper, lower, and exact constraints to restrict the values Solver can choose from to adjust the cells. Using the bicycle example again, you could determine the least and greatest possible number of miles traveled at a given speed and distance.

Here's a summary of when you would use each of these tools:

- Use Goal Seek when you want to find the correct single input value to achieve the desired single output value.

- Use data tables when you want to display the effect of one or two variables on one or more formulas in table format.

- Use scenarios when you want to create, change, and save a number of different sets of values and formulas that each produces different results.

- Use Solver to find the best solution to problems that revolve around the manipulation of several changing cells, variables, and constraints.

System Requirements and Setup

I could have written this book to make it apply to several versions of Excel. Then I could point out everywhere in the text that you would need to adapt for a specific Excel edition. But I thought that approach would be very tedious and confusing to most readers. Therefore, I chose to write this book with Excel 2003 in mind. There are few, if any, differences in the basic user interface and functionality of the what-if tools included in Excel 2003, Excel 2002, Excel 2000, and Excel 97.

In Excel, Goal Seek and scenarios are available on the Tools menu by default. Data tables are available on the Data menu by default. Solver is usually available on the Tools menu. However, if you do not see Solver on the Tools menu, you can add it by clicking Tools ➤ Add-Ins, selecting the Solver Add-In check box, and clicking OK. Note that Excel may ask you to provide your original Excel installation media so that it can locate and install Solver.

After you set up Excel, you can begin working through the Try It exercises provided throughout this book. In all my years both as a communicator and student of technical concepts, I have become a firm believer of the "read it, see it, do it" approach to learning new information. Since that is how I communicate technical concepts, I apply the same approach here.

I start each chapter by sharing a very simple, somewhat light-hearted scenario to get you quickly oriented to each concept. Then I show the concept in a more serious scenario, accompanied by a few notes and tips that you will want to keep in mind as you approach each concept, along with a small number of screen shots for tougher concepts that deserve a picture to help you gain context. Then I let you loose to practice what you have learned with the Try It exercises. If you do not want to spend a lot of time setting up the Try It exercises, you can download them as a series of workbooks from the Source Code area of the Apress web site at `http://www.apress.com`.

What You Should Already Know

As you can probably determine by the book's title, this book is not about teaching you how to use everything in Excel. I assume you already know how to use the basic features of Excel, such as workbooks, worksheets, cells, formulas, menus, and toolbars.

For more information about how to use Excel, see Excel online help (in Excel, click Excel ➤ Microsoft Office Excel Help, or type a question in the Excel Type a Question for Help box, and then press Enter). You can also see Excel online help by visiting the Microsoft Office Online web site at `http://office.microsoft.com`, clicking Assistance, and then clicking Excel 2003.

As with all Internet addresses, there will undoubtedly come a time when the addresses' hosts will change their locations. If you notice a broken Internet address in this book, or any other technical glitch for that matter, please notify us at `http://www.apress.com`. Simply type this book's title in the Search box and click Go. Then click the Submit Errata link.

Getting Started Quicker

Some readers will want to go through this book cover to cover. However, if you want to get started quicker, you can turn to the appendices toward the back of this book. These contain very concise, summarized information, as follows:

- Appendix A, "Excel What-If Tools Quick Start," is a quick way for you to get started after reading just a few pages. While this appendix does not provide in-depth coverage of each what-if feature, it is especially helpful if you need a quick refresher or you get stuck and do not want to reread through an entire book chapter.

- Appendix B, "Summary of Other Helpful Excel Data Analysis Tools," gives you a quick overview of other Excel data analysis tools, such as filtering, sorting, analyzing online analytical processing (OLAP) data, conditional formatting, subtotals, outlining, consolidation, PivotTables, and PivotCharts.

- Appendix C, "Summary of Common Excel Data Analysis Functions," provides a short list of common functions for statistical, mathematical, and financial formulas.

- Appendix D, "Additional Excel Data Analysis Resources," provides several book titles and Internet addresses for further research on various Excel data analysis topics.

Note To read Excel 2003 online help topics about Goal Seek, data tables, scenarios, and Solver, click Help ➤ Microsoft Excel Help ➤ Table of Contents. Expand Working with Data, then Analyzing Data, then Performing What-If Analysis On Worksheet Data.

After you learn some of the basics from these appendices, you can go to the corresponding chapter in this book to learn more.

CHAPTER 1

■ ■ ■

Goal Seek

Goal Seek is a simple, easy-to-use, timesaving tool that enables you to calculate a formula's input value when you want to work backwards from the formula's answer. In this chapter, you will learn more about what Goal Seek is, when you would use Goal Seek, and how to use the Goal Seek dialog box. Then you will work through three Try It exercises to practice goal seeking on your own. The final section in this chapter explains how to troubleshoot common Goal Seek errors.

What Is Goal Seeking?

Goal seeking is the act of finding a specific value for a single worksheet cell by adjusting the value of one other worksheet cell. When you goal seek, Excel adjusts the value in a single worksheet cell that you specify until a formula that is dependent on that worksheet cell returns the result that you want.

For example, say you have two worksheet cells, as shown in Figure 1-1. Cell A1 contains a number referring to a given distance in miles. Cell A2 contains the miles-to-kilometers conversion formula =CONVERT(A1*5280, "ft", "m")/1000. If you enter 10 in cell A1, Excel returns the value of approximately 16.1 in cell A2. But how many miles is 20 kilometers? While you could type one value after another in cell A1 in a trial-and-error fashion (10, 11, 12, 12.5, and so on), until cell A2 displays 20, it's much quicker and more accurate to goal seek. (By the way, the answer is that 20 kilometers is equivalent to about 12.4 miles.)

	A	B
1	10	miles
2	=CONVERT(A1*5280, "ft", "m")/1000	kilometers

Figure 1-1. *Goal seeking for converting miles to kilometers*

When Would I Use Goal Seek?

As you can determine from the previous miles-to-kilometers conversion example, you use the Goal Seek feature when you know the desired result of a single formula, but you do not know the input value the formula needs to determine the result.

You should consider goal seeking when you have a single worksheet cell with a value and another single worksheet cell with a formula that depends on the cell that contains the value, and you want to get to a specific value in the worksheet cell with the formula by adjusting the worksheet cell with the value. For example, say you have two worksheet cells representing a grocery item sales price and the sales price plus 8.8% sales tax. Cell A1 contains the value 5.95, and cell A2 contains the formula =ROUND((A1+(A1*8.8%)), 2), as shown in Figure 1-2. Now you want to know what the grocery item sales price would be if the sales price plus tax were $10.99. Using the Goal Seek feature, you can quickly discover the answer: $10.10.

	A	B
1	5.95	grocery item sales price
2	=ROUND((A1+(A1*8.8%)), 2)	sales price plus tax

Figure 1-2. *Goal seeking for a grocery item sales price plus tax*

As another example, say you have the three worksheet cells shown in Figure 1-3. Cell A1 contains a number referring to a given distance in feet. Cell A2 contains the feet-to-yards conversion formula =CONVERT(A1, "ft", "yd"). Cell A3 contains the yards-to-miles conversion formula =CONVERT(A2, "yd," "mi"). You could goal seek to find out how many feet there are in 1.5 miles (7,920 feet), and you could also goal seek to find out how many miles there are in 3,225 yards (1.83 miles).

	A	B
1	1000	feet
2	=CONVERT(A1, "ft", "yd")	yards
3	=CONVERT(A2, "yd", "mi")	miles

Figure 1-3. *Goal seeking for converting feet to yards to miles*

How Do I Use Goal Seek?

To goal seek in Excel, click Tools ➤ Goal Seek, complete the requested information in the Goal Seek dialog box, and then click OK. The results will appear in the Goal Seek Status dialog box.

The Goal Seek dialog box is simple to use. It consists of three controls: the Set Cell box, the To Value box, and the By Changing Cell box, as shown in Figure 1-4.

Goal Seek	
Set cell:	$A$2
To value:	100
By changing cell:	$A$1
	OK Cancel

Figure 1-4. *The Goal Seek dialog box*

Here's the general procedure for using the Goal Seek dialog box:

1. In the Set Cell box, type or click the reference for the single worksheet cell that contains the formula that you want to set to a desired value.

2. In the To Value box, type the value that you want the cell referred to in the Set Cell box to display.

3. In the By Changing Cell box, type or click the reference for the single worksheet cell that contains the value that you want to adjust. This cell must be referenced by the formula in the cell you specified in the Set Cell box.

After you type or select values for these three boxes, click OK to run Goal Seek. The Goal Seek Status dialog box will appear, reporting whether Excel was able to find a solution. It will also display the target value sought in the To Value box and the current value of the cell in the By Changing Cell box, which may not necessarily match the target value. If Excel does find a solution, the target value and the current value will be equivalent.

For example, say you have two worksheet cells: Cell A1 contains a temperature value in degrees Fahrenheit, and cell A2 contains the Fahrenheit-to-Celsius temperature conversion formula =CONVERT(A1, "F", "C"), as shown in Figure 1-5. Typing 100 in cell A1 returns the Celsius temperature of approximately 37.8 degrees in cell A2. But how many degrees Fahrenheit is a Celsius temperature of 20 degrees?

	A	B
1	100	degrees Fahrenheit
2	=CONVERT(A1, "F", "C")	degrees Celsius

Figure 1-5. *Goal seeking for converting Fahrenheit temperatures to Celsius*

Here's how to figure out the answer:

1. Click Tools ➤ Goal Seek.

2. In the Set Value box, type or click cell A2.

3. In the To Value box, type 20.

4. In the By Changing Cell box, type or click cell A1.

5. Click OK, and click OK again.

The Goal Seek Status dialog box displays the target value, 20, and Excel inserts the answer, 68, into cell A1.

Now that you know how the Goal Seek feature works, practice using it in the following Try It exercises.

Try It: Use Goal Seek to Solve Simple Math Problems

In this exercise, you will use Goal Seek to solve three sets of simple math problems:

- Calculating speed, time, and distance

- Determining circle radius, diameter, circumference, and area

- Using an algebraic equation

These exercises are available in the Excel workbook named Goal Seek Try It Exercises.xls, which is available for download from the Source Code area of the Apress web site (http://www.apress.com). This exercise's math problems are on the workbook's Math Problems worksheet.

Speed, Time, and Distance Math Problems

For your first set of math problems, look at the Math Problem 1 section near the top of the worksheet, as shown in Figure 1-6.

	A	B	C	D	E	F	G	H
1	Math Problem 1: Speed, Time, and Distance							
2								
3	Goal Seeking for Speed			Goal Seeking for Time			Goal Seeking for Distance	
4	=A6*(60/A5)	kilometers per hour		10	kilometers per hour		10	kilometers per hour
5	60	minutes		=D6*(60/D4)	minutes		60	minutes
6	10	kilometers		10	kilometers		=G4*(G5/60)	kilometers

Figure 1-6. *Goal seeking for the speed, time, and distance math problems*

You will goal seek for speed in column A, for time in column D, and for distance in column G. But first, let's review the formulas for these three math problems:

- Speed is calculated in cell A4 as kilometers traveled multiplied by the result of dividing 60 minutes per hour by the number of minutes, or the formula =A6*(60/A5).

- Time is calculated in cell D5 as kilometers multiplied by the result of dividing 60 minutes per hour by the number of kilometers traveled per hour, or the formula =D6*(60/D4).

- Distance is calculated in cell G6 by the number of kilometers traveled multiplied by the number of minutes traveled divided by 60 minutes per hour, or the formula =G4*(G5/60).

Goal Seeking for Speed

For the speed problem, goal seek to determine how many kilometers you would go if you traveled 75 kilometers per hour in 12 minutes.

1. In cell A5, type **12**.

2. Click Tools ➤ Goal Seek.

3. In the Set Cell box, type or click cell **A4**.

4. In the To Value box, type **75**.

5. In the By Changing Cell box, type or click cell **A6**.

6. Click OK, and click OK again.

Answer: You would go 15 kilometers if you traveled 75 kilometers per hour in 12 minutes.

Goal Seeking for Time

For the time problem, goal seek to determine how fast you would go if you traveled 12 kilometers in 8 minutes.

1. In cell D6, type **12**.

2. Click Tools ➤ Goal Seek.

3. In the Set Cell box, type or click cell **D5**.

4. In the To Value box, type **8**.

5. In the By Changing Cell box, type or click cell **D4**.

6. Click OK, and click OK again.

Answer: You would go about 90 kilometers per hour if you traveled 12 kilometers in 8 minutes.

Goal Seeking for Distance

For the distance problem, goal seek to determine how many minutes it would take if you were traveling 85 kilometers at 72 kilometers per hour.

1. In cell G4, type **72**.

2. Click Tools ➤ Goal Seek.

3. In the Set Cell box, type or click cell **G6**.

4. In the To Value box, type **85**.

5. In the By Changing Cell box, type or click cell **G5**.

6. Click OK, and click OK again.

Answer: It would take about 71 minutes if you were traveling 85 kilometers at 72 kilometers per hour.

Circle Radius, Diameter, Circumference, and Area Math Problems

For your second set of math problems, look at the Math Problem 2 section midway down the worksheet, as shown in Figure 1-7.

8	Math Problem 2: Circle Radius, Diameter, Circumference, and Area	
9		
10	4	radius
11	=A10*2	diameter
12	=PI()*A11	circumference
13	=PI()*POWER(A10, 2)	area

Figure 1-7. *Goal seeking for the circle radius, diameter, circumference, and area math problem*

You will goal seek for a circle's diameter, circumference, and area. But first, let's review the formulas for these three math problems:

- Diameter is calculated in cell A11 as twice the radius, or =A10*2.

- Circumference is calculated in cell A12 as the number pi multiplied by the diameter, or =PI()*A11.

- Area is calculated in cell A13 as the number pi multiplied by the square of the radius, or =PI()*POWER(A10, 2).

For these math problems, the units of measurement are unimportant. They could be inches, centimeters, or whatever.

Goal Seeking for the Diameter

For the diameter problem, goal seek to determine the radius when the diameter is 6.25.

1. Click Tools ➤ Goal Seek.

2. In the Set Cell box, type or click cell **A11**.

3. In the To Value box, type **6.25**.

4. In the By Changing Cell box, type or click cell **A10**.

5. Click OK, and click OK again.

Answer: A diameter of 6.25 results in a radius of 3.125.

Goal Seeking for the Circumference

For the circumference problem, goal seek to determine the radius when the circumference is 30.

1. Click Tools ➤ Goal Seek.

2. In the Set Cell box, type or click cell **A12**.

3. In the To Value box, type **30**.

4. In the By Changing Cell box, type or click cell **A10**.

5. Click OK, and click OK again.

Answer: A circumference of 30 results in a radius of about 4.8.

Goal Seeking for the Area

For the area problem, goal seek to determine the radius when the area is 17.

1. Click Tools ➤ Goal Seek.

2. In the Set Cell box, type or click cell **A13**.

3. In the To Value box, type **17**.

4. In the By Changing Cell box, type or click cell **A10**.

5. Click OK, and click OK again.

Answer: An area of 17 results in a radius of about 2.3.

Algebraic Equation Math Problem

For the algebraic equation math problem, look at the Math Problem 3 section toward the bottom of the worksheet, as shown in Figure 1-8.

15	Math Problem 3: Algebraic Equation (ax + by + cz = d)			
16				
17	3	a	4	x
18	3	b	3	y
19	2	c	5	z
20	=(A17*C17)+(A18*C18)+(A19*C19)	d		

Figure 1-8. *Goal seeking for the algebraic equation math problem*

You will goal seek for several variables to produce a desired answer. But first, let's review how this equation works.

Take the algebra expression $ax + by + cz = d$. In this expression, you can substitute all of the values a, b, c, d, x, y, and z, except for one value. Given six of the values, you can determine the seventh value.

Goal Seeking for the Variable C

For the following values:

- a = 1
- b = 2
- d = 12
- x = 1
- y = 2
- z = 1

determine the value of c.

1. Type the following values in the following cells:

   A17: **1**

   A18: **2**

   C17: **1**

   C18: **2**

   C19: **1**

2. Click Tools ➤ Goal Seek.

3. In the Set Cell box, type or click cell **A20**.

4. In the To Value box, type **12**.

5. In the By Changing Cell box, type or click cell **A19**.

6. Click OK, and click OK again.

Answer: If a = 1, b = 2, d = 12, x = 1, y = 2, and z = 1, then c = 7.

Goal Seeking for the Variable Z

For the following values:

- a = 2
- b = 4
- c = 3
- d = 65
- x = 5
- y = 7

determine the value for z.

1. Type the following values in the following cells:

   A17: **2**

   A18: **4**

   A19: **3**

   C17: **5**

   C18: **7**

2. Click Tools ➤ Goal Seek.

3. In the Set Cell box, type or click cell **A20**.

4. In the To Value box, type **65**.

5. In the By Changing Cell box, type or click cell **C19**.

6. Click OK, and click OK again.

Answer: If a = 2, b = 4, c = 3, d = 65, x = 5, and y = 7, then z = 9.

Goal Seeking for the Variable A

For the following values:

- b = 6

- c = 2

- d = 84

- x = 4

- y = 2

- z = 9

determine the value of a.

1. Type the following values in the following cells:

   A18: **6**

   A19: **2**

   C17: **4**

   C18: **2**

   C19: **9**

2. Click Tools ➤ Goal Seek.

3. In the Set Cell box, type or click cell **A20**.

4. In the To Value box, type **84**.

5. In the By Changing Cell box, type or click cell A17.

6. Click OK, and click OK again.

Answer: If b = 6, c = 2, d = 84, x = 4, y = 2, and z = 9, then a = 13.5.

Now that you know how to goal seek with math problems, try goal seeking to forecast interest rates.

Try It: Use Goal Seek to Forecast Interest Rates

In this exercise, you will use Goal Seek to calculate interest rates for a home mortgage, a car loan, and a savings account. These exercises are available on the Goal Seek Try It Exercises.xls file's Interest Rates worksheet.

Home Mortgage Interest Rate

For your first set of interest rate calculations, look at the Interest Rate 1 section near the top of the worksheet, as shown in Figure 1-9.

	A	B
1	Interest Rate 1: Home Mortgage	
2		
3	Loan Amount	200000
4	Term in Months	480
5	Interest Rate	0.0575
6	Monthly Payment	=PMT(B5/12, B4, B3)

Figure 1-9. *Goal seeking for a home mortgage interest rate*

Given a loan amount, a loan term in months, and an interest rate, cell B6 displays the monthly mortgage payment using the function =PMT(Rate, Nper, Pv). In this function, Rate is the interest rate (cell B5 divided by 12), Nper is the total number of payment periods (cell B4), and Pv is the loan's present value (cell B3).

Goal Seeking for the Mortgage Amount

Determine what the loan amount would be given a 15-year term, a 5.75% interest rate, and a $1,100 monthly payment.

1. In cell B4, type **180** (which is 15 years multiplied by 12 months per year). In cell B5, type **5.75%**.

2. Click Tools ➤ Goal Seek.

3. In the Set Cell box, type or click cell **B6**.

4. In the To Value box, type **-1100**.

■Note You use a negative value in the To Value box of the Goal Seek dialog box (which appears on the worksheet as a red number in parentheses) to indicate an outgoing loan payment.

---

5. In the By Changing Cell box, type or click cell **B3**.

6. Click OK, and click OK again.

Answer: The loan amount for a 15-year term, a 5.75% interest rate, and a $1,100 monthly payment is $132,465.

Goal Seeking for the Mortgage Term

Determine what the term would be given a $225,000 loan amount, a 7% interest rate, and a $1,423 monthly payment.

1. In cell B3, type **225000**. In cell B5, type **7%**.

2. Click Tools ➤ Goal Seek.

3. In the Set Cell box, type or click cell **B6**.

4. In the To Value box, type **-1423**.

5. In the By Changing Cell box, type or click cell **B4**.

6. Click OK, and click OK again.

Answer: The term for a $225,000 loan, a 7% interest rate, and a $1,423 monthly payment is about 36.6 years (just over 439 months).

Goal Seeking for the Mortgage Interest Rate

Determine what the interest rate would be given an $850,000 loan amount, a 30-year term, and a $5,225 monthly payment.

1. In cell B3, type **850000**. In cell B4, type **360**.

2. Click Tools ➤ Goal Seek.

3. In the Set Cell box, type or click cell **B6**.

4. In the To Value box, type **-5225**.

5. In the By Changing Cell box, type or click cell **B5**.

6. Click OK, and click OK again.

Answer: The interest rate for an $850,000 loan, a 30-year term, and a $5,225 monthly payment is 6.23%.

Car Loan Interest Rate

For your second set of interest rate calculations, look at the Interest Rate 2 section midway down the worksheet, as shown in Figure 1-10.

8	Interest Rate 2: Car Loan	
9		
10	Loan Amount	9999
11	Interest Rate	0.009
12	Monthly Payment	=PMT(B11/12, B13, B10)
13	Number of Months to Pay Off	72

Figure 1-10. *Goal seeking for a car loan interest rate*

Given a car loan amount, an interest rate, and the number of months to pay off the loan, cell B12 displays the monthly payment using the PMT(Rate, Nper, Pv) function, as in the prior home mortgage interest rate examples. To review, in the PMT function, Rate is the interest rate (cell B11 divided by 12), Nper is the total number of months to pay off the loan (cell B13), and Pv is the loan's present value (cell B10).

Goal Seeking for the Loan Amount

Determine what the loan amount would be given a 2.9% interest rate, a $139.50 monthly payment, and a 6-year term.

1. In cell B11, type **2.9%**. In cell B13, type **72**.

2. Click Tools ➤ Goal Seek.

3. In the Set Cell box, type or click cell **B12**.

4. In the To Value box, type **-139.50**.

5. In the By Changing Cell box, type or click cell **B10**.

6. Click OK, and click OK again.

Answer: The loan amount for a 2.9% interest rate, a $139.50 monthly payment, and a 6-year term is $9,208.54.

Goal Seeking for the Loan Term

Determine what the term would be given an $18,000 loan amount, a 1.7% interest rate, and a $325.00 monthly payment.

1. In cell B10, type **18000**. In cell B11, type **1.7%**.

2. Click Tools ➤ Goal Seek.

3. In the Set Cell box, type or click cell **B12**.

4. In the To Value box, type **-325**.

5. In the By Changing Cell box, type or click cell **B13**.

6. Click OK, and click OK again.

Answer: The term for an $18,000 loan amount, a 1.7% interest rate, and a $325.00 monthly payment is 58 months.

Goal Seeking for the Loan Interest Rate

Determine what the interest rate would be given a $12,999 loan amount, a 5-year term, and a $239.00 monthly payment.

1. In cell B10, type **12999**. In cell B13, type **60**.

2. Click Tools ➤ Goal Seek.

3. In the Set Cell box, type or click cell **B12**.

4. In the To Value box, type **-239**.

5. In the By Changing Cell box, type or click cell **B11**.

6. Click OK, and click OK again.

Answer: The interest rate for a $12,999 loan, a 5-year term, and a $239.00 monthly payment is 3.93%.

Savings Account Interest Rate

For your third set of interest rate calculations, look at the Interest Rate 3 section toward the bottom of the worksheet, as shown in Figure 1-11.

16	Interest Rate 3: Savings Account	
17		
18	Initial Investment	2500
19	Months Invested	48
20	Interest Rate	0.0311
21	Ending Amount	=FV(B20/12, B19, ,-B18)

Figure 1-11. *Goal seeking for a savings account interest rate*

Given an initial investment, the number of months the investment remains untouched, and an unchanged interest rate, cell B21 displays the investment's ending value using the function =FV(Rate, Nper, , -Pv). The FV function is similar to the PMT function you used in the previous examples, except that the investment's present value must be expressed as an inverse of its initial investment value.

Goal Seeking for the Initial Investment Amount

Determine what the initial investment would be given a 10-year investment term, a 1.75% interest rate, and a $15,000 ending value.

1. In cell B19, type **120**. In cell B20, type **1.75%**.

2. Click Tools ➤ Goal Seek.

3. In the Set Cell box, type or click cell **B21**.

4. In the To Value box, type **15000**.

5. In the By Changing Cell box, type or click cell **B18**.

6. Click OK, and click OK again.

Answer: The initial investment for a 10-year investment term, a 1.75% interest rate, and a $15,000 ending value is $12,593.46.

Goal Seeking for the Investment Term

Determine what the investment term would be given a $5,000 initial investment, a 3.25% interest rate, and a $7,200 ending value.

1. In cell B18, type **5000**. In cell B20, type **3.25%**.

2. Click Tools ➤ Goal Seek.

3. In the Set Cell box, type or click cell **B21**.

4. In the To Value box, type **7200**.

5. In the By Changing Cell box, type or click cell **B19**.

6. Click OK, and click OK again.

Answer: The investment term for a $5,000 initial investment, a 3.25% interest rate, and a $7,200 ending value is about 11.25 years (about 135 months).

Goal Seeking for the Investment Interest Rate

Determine the interest rate given a $25,000 initial investment, a 5-year term, and a $30,000 ending value.

1. In cell B18, type **25000**. In cell B19, type **60**.

2. Click Tools ➤ Goal Seek.

3. In the Set Cell box, type or click cell **B21**.

4. In the To Value box, type **30000**.

5. In the By Changing Cell box, type or click cell **B20**.

6. Click OK, and click OK again.

Answer: The interest rate for a $25,000 initial investment, a 5-year term, and a $30,000 ending value is 3.65%.

Now that you can goal seek to forecast interest rates, try goal seeking with a real-world business profitability scenario.

Try It: Use Goal Seek to Determine Optimal Ticket Prices

Now, you will use the Goal Seek feature to determine the best ticket prices and number of tickets to sell at those prices for a theater to achieve a desired box office income amount. These exercises are available on the Goal Seek Try It Exercises.xls file's Theater Ticket Prices worksheet, as shown in Figure 1-12.

	A	B	C
1		Price Per Ticket	Tickets to Sell
2	Child Ticket	3	75
3	Adult Ticket	5	125
4	Senior Ticket	4	105
5			
6	Box Office Income	=(B2*C2)+(B3*C3)+(B4*C4)	

Figure 1-12. *Goal seeking for optimal theater ticket prices*

The worksheet is simple to understand. It contains three ticket price points for child, adult, and senior tickets. The target box office income is the sum of the child, adult, and senior tickets multiplied by their respective number of tickets to sell.

Number of Tickets Sold

In this first set of exercises, you will goal seek to find the number of child, adult, and senior tickets that you need to sell to achieve a specified box office income.

Goal Seeking for the Number of Child Tickets Sold

Determine how many child tickets would need to be sold at $3.25 assuming a box office income of $3,000, 225 adult tickets sold at $6.50, and 100 senior tickets sold at $4.75.

1. Type the following values in the following cells:

    B2: **3.25**

    B3: **6.5**

    C3: **225**

    B4: **4.75**

    C4: **100**

2. Click Tools ➤ Goal Seek.

3. In the Set Cell box, type or click cell **B6**.

4. In the To Value box, type **3000**.

5. In the By Changing Cell box, type or click cell **C2**.

6. Click OK, and click OK again.

Answer: The number of child tickets that would need to be sold at $3.25 assuming a box office income of $3,000, 225 adult tickets sold at $6.50, and 100 senior tickets sold at $4.75 is about 327.

Goal Seeking for the Number of Adult Tickets Sold

Determine how many adult tickets would need to be sold at $6.50 assuming a box office income of $2,500, 200 child tickets sold at $3.00, and 75 senior tickets sold at $4.50.

1. Type the following values in the following cells:

   B2: **3**

   C2: **200**

   B3: **6.5**

   B4: **4.5**

   C4: **75**

2. Click Tools ➤ Goal Seek.

3. In the Set Cell box, type or click cell **B6**.

4. In the To Value box, type **2500**.

5. In the By Changing Cell box, type or click cell **C3**.

6. Click OK, and click OK again.

Answer: The number of adult tickets that would need to be sold at $6.50 assuming a box office income of $2,500, 200 child tickets sold at $3.00, and 75 senior tickets sold at $4.50 is about 240.

Goal Seeking for the Number of Senior Tickets Sold

Determine how many senior tickets would need to be sold at $4.25 assuming a box office income of $2,750, 175 child tickets sold at $3.50, and 250 adult tickets sold at $7.00.

1. Type the following values in the following cells:

   B2: **3.5**

   C2: **175**

   B3: **7**

   C3: **250**

   B4: **4.25**

2. Click Tools ➤ Goal Seek.

3. In the Set Cell box, type or click cell **B6**.

4. In the To Value box, type **2750**.

5. In the By Changing Cell box, type or click cell **C4**.

6. Click OK, and click OK again.

Answer: The number of senior tickets that would need to be sold at $4.25 assuming a box office income of $2,750, 175 child tickets sold at $3.50, and 250 adult tickets sold at $7.00 is about 91.

Ticket Prices

In this next set of exercises, you will goal seek to find the amount to charge for child, adult, and senior tickets to achieve a specified box office income.

Goal Seeking for the Child Ticket Price

Determine how much to charge per child ticket assuming 150 child tickets sold, a box office income of $2,750, 250 adult tickets sold at $6.00, and 150 senior tickets sold at $5.00.

1. Type the following values in the following cells:

> C2: **150**
>
> B3: **6**
>
> C3: **250**
>
> B4: **5**
>
> C4: **150**

2. Click Tools ➤ Goal Seek.

3. In the Set Cell box, type or click cell **B6**.

4. In the To Value box, type **2750**.

5. In the By Changing Cell box, type or click cell **B2**.

6. Click OK, and click OK again.

Answer: The amount to charge per child ticket assuming 150 child tickets sold, a box office income of $2,750, 250 adult tickets sold at $6.00, and 150 senior tickets sold at $5.00 is $3.33.

Goal Seeking for the Adult Ticket Price

Determine how much to charge per adult ticket assuming 125 adult tickets sold, a box office income of $2,500, 200 child tickets sold at $4.00, and 110 senior tickets sold at $5.75.

1. Type the following values in the following cells:

> B2: **4**
>
> C2: **200**
>
> C3: **125**
>
> B4: **5.75**
>
> C4: **110**

2. Click Tools ➤ Goal Seek.

3. In the Set Cell box, type or click cell **B6**.

4. In the To Value box, type **2500**.

5. In the By Changing Cell box, type or click cell **B3**.

6. Click OK, and click OK again.

Answer: The amount to charge per adult ticket assuming 125 adult tickets sold, a box office income of $2,500, 200 child tickets sold at $4.00, and 110 senior tickets sold at $5.75 is $8.54.

Goal Seeking for the Senior Ticket Price

Determine how much to charge per senior ticket assuming 225 senior tickets sold, a box office income of $4,000, 175 child tickets sold at $5.00, and 200 adult tickets sold at $7.50.

1. Type the following values in the following cells:

B2: **5**

C2: **175**

B3: **7.5**

C3: **200**

C4: **225**

2. Click Tools ➤ Goal Seek.

3. In the Set Cell box, type or click cell **B6**.

4. In the To Value box, type **4000**.

5. In the By Changing Cell box, type or click cell **B4**.

6. Click OK, and click OK again.

Answer: The amount to charge per senior ticket assuming 225 senior tickets sold, a box office income of $4,000, 175 child tickets sold at $5.00, and 200 adult tickets sold at $7.50 is $7.22.

■**Note** You can also use Solver for the theater ticket price problems. You will revisit this example in Chapter 4, which covers Solver.

Troubleshooting Goal Seek

When you click the Goal Seek dialog box's OK button to run a goal seek calculation, you may see one of the following error messages instead of the results:

Cell Must Contain a Formula: This error message appears when the worksheet cell referred to in the Set Cell box does not contain a formula. This error commonly occurs when you accidentally confuse the cell reference for the Set Cell box with the cell reference for the By Changing cell box. To fix this problem, type or select a cell that contains a formula in the Set Cell box, and then click OK again.

Your Entry Cannot Be Used. An Integer or Decimal Number May Be Required: This error message appears when you type one or more alphanumeric characters that Excel does not recognize as a number in the To Value box. To fix this problem, type an integer or decimal number in the To Value box, and then click OK again.

Cell Must Contain a Value: This error message appears when the worksheet cell referred to in the By Changing Cell box does not contain a value. This error commonly occurs when you accidentally confuse the cell reference for the By Changing Cell box with the cell reference for the Set Cell box. To fix this problem, type or select a cell that contains a value in the By Changing Cell box, and then click OK again.

Reference Is Not Valid: This error message appears when Excel does not recognize the contents of either the Set Cell box or By Changing Cell box as a valid worksheet cell refer- ence. This error commonly occurs when you incorrectly type the worksheet cell reference instead of clicking the desired cell on the worksheet. To fix this problem, type or select a valid worksheet cell reference for the Set Cell and By Changing Cell boxes, and then click OK again.

Goal Seeking with Cell [Cell Reference] May Not Have Found a Solution: This message appears when Excel is not confident that it found a value that matched the Goal Seek dialog box's To Value box. This message commonly appears when you type a number in the To Value box that is extremely large or extremely small. To address this message, click the Goal Seek Status dialog box's Cancel button, click Tools ➤ Goal Seek, type a different number in the To Value box, and click OK.

Summary

In this chapter, you learned how to use Goal Seek, an easy-to-use timesaving tool that helps you figure out a formula's input value when you are given only the formula's answer. You prac- ticed using Goal Seek by working through three Try It exercises. Finally, you saw what error messages might appear when you're using Goal Seek and how to fix the associated problems.

CHAPTER 2

■■■

Data Tables

Data tables are a handy way to display the results of multiple formula calculations in an at-a-glance lookup format. In this chapter, you will learn more about what data tables are, when you would want to use data tables, and how to create data tables. Then you will work through three Try It exercises to practice creating data tables on your own. The final section covers troubleshooting common problems with data tables.

What Are Data Tables?

A *data table* is a collection of cells that displays how changing values in worksheet formulas affects the results of those formulas. Data tables provide a convenient way to calculate, display, and compare multiple outcomes of a given formula in a single operation.

For example, Figure 2-1 illustrates a Fahrenheit-to-Celsius conversion table. In this data table, cells A3 through A71 list the numbers 32 to 100 in degrees Fahrenheit, and cells B3 through B71 list the corresponding numbers 0 to 37.8 in degrees Celsius. Cell A3 contains the number 32 (for the Fahrenheit value), and cell B3 contains the number 0 (for the Celsius value); cell A4 contains 33, and cell B4 contains 0.6; and so on. To determine how many degrees Celsius 96 degrees Fahrenheit is, simply look at cell B67 to find the answer: 35.6 degrees Celsius.

	A	B	C	D
1		100	Degrees Fahrenheit	
2		37.8	Degrees Celsius	
3	32	0.0		
4	33	0.6		
5	34	1.1		
6	35	1.7		
7	36	2.2		
66	95	35.0		
67	96	35.6		
68	97	36.1		
69	98	36.7		
70	99	37.2		
71	100	37.8		

Figure 2-1. *A Fahrenheit-to-Celsius conversion table (panes split for readability)*

■**Note** You don't need to type the values in cells B3 to B71. To create the data table in Figure 2-1, you provide the known values in cells A3 through A71 and the formula in cell B2 (which, in this case, is =CONVERT(B1, "F", "C")). Excel automatically calculates the values in cells B3 through B71.

As another example, Figure 2-2 shows a multiplication table, which lists the products of multiplicands between the numbers 1 and 13. Cells A4 through A16 list the numbers 1 through 13, while cells B3 through N3 list the numbers 1 through 13 as well. The intersection of any of these two sets of numbers displays the product of those two numbers. So, the intersection of the number 7 in cell A10 and the number 9 in cell J3 produces the result, 63, in cell J10. Similarly, the intersection of the number 11 in cell A14 and the number 12 in cell M3 produces the result, 132, in cell M14.

	A	B	C	D	E	F	G	H	I	J	K	L	M	N
1	1													
2	1													
3	1	1	2	3	4	5	6	7	8	9	10	11	12	13
4	1	1	2	3	4	5	6	7	8	9	10	11	12	13
5	2	2	4	6	8	10	12	14	16	18	20	22	24	26
6	3	3	6	9	12	15	18	21	24	27	30	33	36	39
7	4	4	8	12	16	20	24	28	32	36	40	44	48	52
8	5	5	10	15	20	25	30	35	40	45	50	55	60	65
9	6	6	12	18	24	30	36	42	48	54	60	66	72	78
10	7	7	14	21	28	35	42	49	56	63	70	77	84	91
11	8	8	16	24	32	40	48	56	64	72	80	88	96	104
12	9	9	18	27	36	45	54	63	72	81	90	99	108	117
13	10	10	20	30	40	50	60	70	80	90	100	110	120	130
14	11	11	22	33	44	55	66	77	88	99	110	121	132	143
15	12	12	24	36	48	60	72	84	96	108	120	132	144	156
16	13	13	26	39	52	65	78	91	104	117	130	143	156	169

Figure 2-2. *A multiplication table*

In both of these examples, you can think of a data table as a lookup table. Looking up 98 degrees Fahrenheit in cell A69 of the data table in Figure 2-1 reveals the result of 36.7 degrees Celsius (in cell B69). Similarly, looking up the product of 8 and 9 in cell J11 of the data table in Figure 2-2, which is the intersection of cells A11 and J3, is 72.

When Would I Use Data Tables?

You use data tables when you want a convenient way to represent the results of running several iterations of a formula using various inputs to that formula.

For example, you may want to provide a data table listing retail sales prices and their equivalent sales prices with sales tax added, as shown in Figure 2-3. Cells A3 through A102 list whole dollar amounts from $1.00 to $100.00, while cells B3 through B102 list the corresponding whole dollar amounts with sales tax added. So, if the sales tax rate were 8.8%, cell A3 would display $1.00, and cell B3 would display $1.09. Similarly, cell A99 would display $97.00, and cell B99 would display $105.54.

	A	B	C	D
1		$1.00	Sales price	
2		$1.09	Sales price with 8.8% tax	
3	$1.00	$1.09		
4	$2.00	$2.18		
5	$3.00	$3.27		
6	$4.00	$4.36		
7	$5.00	$5.44		
97	$95.00	$103.36		
98	$96.00	$104.45		
99	$97.00	$105.54		
100	$98.00	$106.63		
101	$99.00	$107.72		
102	$100.00	$108.80		

Figure 2-3. *A data table listing retail sales prices with and without sales tax added (panes split for readability)*

Going further with this example, you may want to provide a data table listing the same retail prices, but with various discount percentages applied and their equivalent discounted sales prices with sales tax added after that, as shown in Figure 2-4. Cells B4 through B103 list whole dollar amounts from $1.00 to $100.00 as before, but cells C3 through V3 list discount percentages in 5% increments, from 0% to 95%. So, cell B4 would still display $1.00, while cell T4 (an 85% discount) would display $0.17. Similarly, cell A99 would still display $96.00, while cell E99 (a 10% discount) would display $94.01.

	A	B	C	D	E	T	U	V
1	Sales price	$1.00						
2	Sales discount	5%						
3	Then add 8.8% tax	$1.04	0%	5%	10%	85%	90%	95%
4			$1.00	$1.09	$1.04	$0.98	$0.17	$0.11	$0.06
5			$2.00	$2.18	$2.07	$1.96	$0.33	$0.22	$0.11
6			$3.00	$3.27	$3.11	$2.94	$0.49	$0.33	$0.17
7			$4.00	$4.36	$4.14	$3.92	$0.66	$0.44	$0.22
8			$5.00	$5.44	$5.17	$4.90	$0.82	$0.55	$0.28
98			$95.00	$103.36	$98.20	$93.03	$15.51	$10.34	$5.17
99			$96.00	$104.45	$99.23	$94.01	$15.67	$10.45	$5.23
100			$97.00	$105.54	$100.26	$94.99	$15.84	$10.56	$5.28
101			$98.00	$106.63	$101.30	$95.97	$16.00	$10.67	$5.34
102			$99.00	$107.72	$102.33	$96.95	$16.16	$10.78	$5.39
103			$100.00	$108.80	$103.36	$97.92	$16.32	$10.88	$5.44

Figure 2-4. *A data table listing retail sales prices with discounts and sales tax added (panes split for readability)*

How Do I Create Data Tables?

To create data tables, you need to understand the two types of data tables. You should also be familiar with how data tables are constructed with input and output data in various worksheet cells.

You can create either *one-variable* or *two-variable* data tables. The difference is in the number of *input values* contained in the table. In a one-variable data table, input values consist of one *input cell*. In a two-variable data table, input values consist of two input cells. These input cells contain the replaceable values in the formula that are substituted from the row or column input values (for one-variable data tables) or the row and column input values (for two-variable data tables).

Data tables also contain *result values*. Result values are, as the name suggests, the results of substituting the input values in the formula.

For example, in the data table in Figure 2-5, cells B1 and B2 are the input cells, cells B4 through B13 are the column input values, cells C3 through L3 are the row input values, and cells C4 through L13 (the cells with the values 1.4 through 14.1) are the result values.

	A	B	C	D	E	F	G	H	I	J	K	L
1	a squared	1		The Pythagorean Theorem (a2 + b2 = c2)								
2	b squared	1										
3	square root of c	1.4	1	2	3	4	5	6	7	8	9	10
4			1	1.4	2.2	3.2	4.1	5.1	6.1	7.1	8.1	9.1	10.0
5			2	2.2	2.8	3.6	4.5	5.4	6.3	7.3	8.2	9.2	10.2
6			3	3.2	3.6	4.2	5.0	5.8	6.7	7.6	8.5	9.5	10.4
7			4	4.1	4.5	5.0	5.7	6.4	7.2	8.1	8.9	9.8	10.8
8			5	5.1	5.4	5.8	6.4	7.1	7.8	8.6	9.4	10.3	11.2
9			6	6.1	6.3	6.7	7.2	7.8	8.5	9.2	10.0	10.8	11.7
10			7	7.1	7.3	7.6	8.1	8.6	9.2	9.9	10.6	11.4	12.2
11			8	8.1	8.2	8.5	8.9	9.4	10.0	10.6	11.3	12.0	12.8
12			9	9.1	9.2	9.5	9.8	10.3	10.8	11.4	12.0	12.7	13.5
13			10	10.0	10.2	10.4	10.8	11.2	11.7	12.2	12.8	13.5	14.1

Figure 2-5. *A data table listing values according to the Pythagorean Theorem, where $a^2 + b^2 = c^2$*

Now that you understand data tables terminology, you will learn how to work with one-variable and two-variable data tables.

Working with One-Variable Data Tables

You must organize the data on your worksheets in a certain way in order for Excel to properly create data tables. You design one-variable data tables so that input values are listed either down a column or across a row. A formula used in a one-variable data table must refer to a single input cell.

Here's the general procedure for setting up and creating a one-variable data table:

1. Type the formula in the appropriate location:

   - If the input values are listed down a column, type the formula in the row above the first column value, and then one cell to the right of the column of values.

   - If the input values are listed across a row, type the formula in the column one cell below the row of values.

2. Select the group of cells that contains the formula and input values that you want to substitute.

3. Click Data ➤ Table.

4. Identify the input cell reference:

   - If the input values are listed down a column, type or click the input cell reference in the Column Input box.

   - If the input values are listed across a row, type or click the input cell reference in the Row Input box.

5. Click OK.

For example, Figure 2-6 shows how to set up a one-variable data table with input values down a column. Notice that the formula is in the cell above and then to the right of the first column input value. Cell B1 and cells A3 through A12 contain the number of free airline trips. Cell B2 holds the formula =B1*25000. The data table automatically calculates the values in cells B3 through B12.

	A	B	C
1		1	number of free airline trips
2		25,000	number of miles flown to earn those trips
3	1	25,000	
4	2	50,000	
5	3	75,000	
6	4	100,000	
7	5	125,000	
8	6	150,000	
9	7	175,000	
10	8	200,000	
11	9	225,000	
12	10	250,000	

Figure 2-6. *Setting up a one-variable data table with input values down a column*

Figure 2-7 shows how to set up a one-variable data table with input values across a row. Notice that the formula is in the cell below the first row input value. Cells B1 through K1 contain the number of free airline trips. Cell B2 contains the formula =B1*25000. The data table automatically calculates the values in cells C2 through K2.

	A	B	C	D	I	J	K
1	number of free airline trips	1	2	3	8	9	10
2	number of miles flown to earn those trips	25,000	50,000	75,000	200,000	225,000	250,000

Figure 2-7. *Setting up a one-variable data table with input values across a row (panes split for readability)*

Working with Two-Variable Data Tables

Unlike one-variable data tables, two-variable data tables' input values are listed both down a column and across a row. A formula used in a two-variable data table refers to two different input cells.

Here's the general procedure for setting up and creating a two-variable data table:

1. Type the formula that will serve as the basis of the two-variable data table.

2. Type the list of column input values below the formula in the same column.

3. Type the list of row input values in the same row as the formula, just to the right of the formula.

4. Select the group of cells that contains the formula and the column and row of input values that you want to substitute.

5. Click Data ➤ Table.

6. In the Column Input box, type or click the column input cell reference.

7. In the Row Input box, type or click the row input cell reference.

8. Click OK.

For example, Figure 2-8 shows how to set up a two-variable data table. In this example, the formula is the sum of basketball free throws and field goals made multiplied by the points for each free throw and field goal. Notice that the list of column input values begins below the formula in the same column as the formula. The list of row input values begins in the same row as the formula, just to the right of the formula.

	B4	▼	*fx*	=(B2*2)+B3									
	A	B	C	D	E	F	G	H	I	J	K	L	M
1	Basketball statistics												
2	Field goals	3											
3	Free throws	8											
4	Total points	14	1	2	3	4	5	6	7	8	9	10	Free throws
5		1	3	4	5	6	7	8	9	10	11	12	
6		2	5	6	7	8	9	10	11	12	13	14	
7		3	7	8	9	10	11	12	13	14	15	16	
8		4	9	10	11	12	13	14	15	16	17	18	
9		5	11	12	13	14	15	16	17	18	19	20	
10		6	13	14	15	16	17	18	19	20	21	22	
11		7	15	16	17	18	19	20	21	22	23	24	
12		8	17	18	19	20	21	22	23	24	25	26	
13		9	19	20	21	22	23	24	25	26	27	28	
14		10	21	22	23	24	25	26	27	28	29	30	
15		Field goals											

Figure 2-8. *Setting up a two-variable data table*

Clearing Data Tables

After you create a data table, you may discover that you entered the wrong input cell references, and you want to re-create the data table. Here's how to do this:

1. Select all of the data table's result values.

2. Click Edit ➤ Clear ➤ Contents.

3. Create the data table again.

If you want to clear an entire data table, including the formula, the input cells, the input values, and the result values, follow these steps:

1. Select the entire data table, including all formulas, input cells, input values, and result values.

2. Click Edit ➤ Clear ➤ All.

Converting Data Tables

You may want to convert formula result values into constant values (in other words, to remove the formulas from result value cells). Here's how to do this:

1. Select all of the data table's result values.

2. Click Edit ➤ Copy.

3. Click Edit ➤ Paste Special.

4. Click the Values option.

5. Click OK.

6. Press Enter.

Adjusting Data Table Calculation Options

If you recalculate the values in a workbook and the workbook contains data tables, by default, the data tables' result values will be recalculated as well, even if the result values themselves have not changed. This results in slower overall recalculation performance for the workbook. To speed up recalculations for a workbook that contains data tables, follow these steps:

1. Click Tools ➤ Options, and then click the Calculation tab.

2. Click the Automatic Except Tables option.

3. Click OK.

■**Note** To manually recalculate a data table later, click the data table's formula, and then press F9 (to recalculate all worksheets in all open workbooks) or press Shift+F9 (to recalculate only the active worksheet).

Now that you know how to create data tables, practice using them in the following Try It exercises.

Try It: Use Data Tables to Forecast Savings Account Details

In this exercise, you will use one-variable and two-variable data tables to forecast savings account financial details. These exercises are included in the Excel workbook named Data Tables Try It Exercises.xls, which is available for download from the Source Code area of the Apress web site (http://www.apress.com). This exercise's data tables are on the workbook's One-Variable Interest Rates and Two-Variable Interest Rates worksheets.

Notice that on these two worksheets, cells B1 through B4 contain the initial input data, as follows:

- Cell B1 represents the initial savings account investment.

- Cell B2 represents the interest rate, compounded monthly.

- Cell B3 represents the savings term in months.

- Cell B4 represents the ending savings account value, expressed using the function =FV(Rate, Nper, , Pv). In this function, Rate is the interest rate (cell B2 divided by 12), Nper is the total number of payment periods (cell B3), and Pv is the savings account's present value (cell B1).

One-Variable Data Table to Forecast Savings Account Details

To create the one-variable data table, start with the data on the One-Variable Interest Rates worksheet, as shown in Figure 2-9.

	A	B
1	Initial Investment	100
2	Interest Rate, Compounded Monthly	0.023
3	Term (Months)	12
4	Ending Value	=FV(B2/12, B3, , -B1)

Figure 2-9. *Initial data before creating the one-variable data table to forecast savings account financial details*

Next, determine what the ending savings account value would be for initial investment amounts of $100.00 to $1,000.00, in $100.00 increments. Do the following to create the data table and format the results:

1. In cell A5, type **100**.

2. Select cells A5 through A14.

3. Click Edit ➤ Fill ➤ Series.

4. In the Step Value box, type **100**.

5. Click OK.

6. Select cells A4 through B14.

7. Click Data ➤ Table.

8. In the Column Input Cell box, type or click cell **B1**.

9. Click OK.

10. Select cells A5 through B14.

11. Click Format ➤ Cells.

12. Click Currency in the Category list.

13. Click OK.

Compare your results to Figure 2-10.

	A	B
1	Initial Investment	$100.00
2	Compounded	2.30%
3	Term (Months)	12
4	Ending Value	$102.32
5	$100.00	$102.32
6	$200.00	$204.65
7	$300.00	$306.97
8	$400.00	$409.30
9	$500.00	$511.62
10	$600.00	$613.95
11	$700.00	$716.27
12	$800.00	$818.60
13	$900.00	$920.92
14	$1,000.00	$1,023.24

Figure 2-10. *Completed one-variable data table to forecast savings account financial details*

Two-Variable Data Table to Forecast Savings Account Details

To create the two-variable data table, start with the data on the Two-Variable Interest Rates worksheet. The initial data looks just like the data in the One-Variable Interest Rates worksheet, shown earlier in Figure 2-9.

Next, determine what the ending savings account value would be for initial investment amounts of $100.00 to $1,000.00, in $100.00 increments and savings terms of 12 months to 60 months. Do the following to create the data table and format the results:

1. In cell B5, type **100**.

2. Select cells B5 through B14.

3. Click Edit ➤ Fill ➤ Series.

4. In the Step Value box, type **100**.

5. Click OK.

6. In cell C4, type **12**.

7. Select cells C4 through G4.

8. Click Edit ➤ Fill ➤ Series.

9. In the Step Value box, type **12**.

10. Click OK.

11. Select cells B4 through G14.

12. Click Data ➤ Table.

13. In the Row Input Cell box, type or click cell **B3**.

14. In the Column Input Cell box, type or click cell **B1**.

15. Click OK.

16. Select cells B5 through G14.

17. Click Format ➤ Cells.

18. Click Currency in the Category list.

19. Click OK.

Compare your results to Figure 2-11.

	A	B	C	D	E	F	G
1	Initial Investment	$100.00					
2	Interest Rate, Compounded Monthly	2.30%					
3	Term (Months)	12					
4	Ending Value	$102.32	12	24	36	48	60
5		$100.00	$102.32	$104.70	$107.14	$109.63	$112.17
6		$200.00	$204.65	$209.41	$214.27	$219.25	$224.35
7		$300.00	$306.97	$314.11	$321.41	$328.88	$336.52
8		$400.00	$409.30	$418.81	$428.55	$438.51	$448.70
9		$500.00	$511.62	$523.51	$535.68	$548.13	$560.87
10		$600.00	$613.95	$628.22	$642.82	$657.76	$673.05
11		$700.00	$716.27	$732.92	$749.96	$767.39	$785.22
12		$800.00	$818.60	$837.62	$857.09	$877.01	$897.40
13		$900.00	$920.92	$942.33	$964.23	$986.64	$1,009.57
14		$1,000.00	$1,023.24	$1,047.03	$1,071.37	$1,096.27	$1,121.75

Figure 2-11. *Completed two-variable data table to forecast savings account financial details*

Now try using one-variable and two-variable data tables to determine artist royalty payments.

Try It: Use Data Tables to Determine Royalty Payments

In this exercise, you will create one-variable and two-variable data tables to determine music artist royalty payments. These exercises are available on the Data Tables Try It Exercises.xls workbook's One-Variable Royalty Payments and Two-Variable Royalty Payments worksheets.

Notice that on these two worksheets, cells B1 through B5 contain the initial input data, as follows:

- Cell B1 represents the recording units' suggested retail price.

- Cell B2 represents the units' wholesale price expressed as a percentage of the suggested retail price.

- Cell B3 represents the artist's royalty rate expressed as a percentage.

- Cell B4 represents the number of recording units sold.

- Cell B5 represents the artist's royalty, using the simple formula B1*B2*B3*B4.

One-Variable Data Table to Determine Royalty Payments

To create the one-variable data table, start with the data on the One-Variable Royalty Payments worksheet, as shown in Figure 2-12.

	A	B
1	Suggested Retail Price	14.99
2	Wholesale Price	0.6
3	Artist Royalty Rate	0.067
4	Units Sold	5000
5	Artist Royalty	=B1*B2*B3*B4

Figure 2-12. *Initial data before creating the one-variable data table to determine artist royalty payments*

Next, determine what the artist's royalty payments would be for recording units sold of 10,000 to 100,000, in 10,000-unit increments. Do the following to create the data table and format the results:

1. In cell A6, type **10000**.

2. Select cells A6 through A15.

3. Click Edit ➤ Fill ➤ Series.

4. In the Step Value box, type **10000**.

5. Click OK.

6. Select cells A5 through B15.

7. Click Data ➤ Table.

8. In the Column Input Cell box, type or click cell **B4**.

9. Click OK.

10. Select cells B6 through B15.

11. Click Format ➤ Cells.

12. Click Currency in the Category list.

13. Click OK.

Compare your results to Figure 2-13.

	A	B
1	Suggested Retail Price	$14.99
2	Wholesale Price	60%
3	Artist Royalty Rate	6.7%
4	Units Sold	5,000
5	Artist Royalty	$3,012.99
6	10,000	$6,025.98
7	20,000	$12,051.96
8	30,000	$18,077.94
9	40,000	$24,103.92
10	50,000	$30,129.90
11	60,000	$36,155.88
12	70,000	$42,181.86
13	80,000	$48,207.84
14	90,000	$54,233.82
15	100,000	$60,259.80

Figure 2-13. *Completed one-variable data table to determine artist royalty payments*

Two-Variable Data Table to Determine Royalty Payments

To create the two-variable data table, start with the data on the Two-Variable Royalty Payments worksheet. The initial data looks just like the data in the One-Variable Royalty Payments worksheet, shown earlier in Figure 2-12.

Next, determine what the artist's royalty payments would be for recording units sold of 10,000 to 100,000, in 10,000-unit increments and artist royalty percentages from 8% to 10% in 0.5% increments. Do the following to create the data table and format the results:

1. In cell B6, type **10000**.

2. Select cells B6 through B15.

3. Click Edit ➤ Fill ➤ Series.

4. In the Step Value box, type **10000**.

5. Click OK.

6. Type the following values in the following cells:

   C5: **8.0%**

   D5: **8.5%**

   E5: **9.0%**

   F5: **9.5%**

   G5: **10.0%**

7. Select cells B5 through G15.

8. Click Data ➤ Table.

9. In the Row Input Cell box, type or click cell **B3**.

10. In the Column Input Cell box, type or click cell **B4**.

11. Click OK.

12. Select cells C6 through G15.

13. Click Format ➤ Cells.

14. Click Currency in the Category list.

15. Click OK.

Compare your results to Figure 2-14.

	A	B	C	D	E	F	G
1	Suggested Retail Price	$14.99					
2	Wholesale Price	60%					
3	Artist Royalty Rate	6.7%					
4	Units Sold	5,000					
5	Artist Royalty	$3,012.99	8.0%	8.5%	9.0%	9.5%	10.0%
6		10,000	$7,195.20	$7,644.90	$8,094.60	$8,544.30	$8,994.00
7		20,000	$14,390.40	$15,289.80	$16,189.20	$17,088.60	$17,988.00
8		30,000	$21,585.60	$22,934.70	$24,283.80	$25,632.90	$26,982.00
9		40,000	$28,780.80	$30,579.60	$32,378.40	$34,177.20	$35,976.00
10		50,000	$35,976.00	$38,224.50	$40,473.00	$42,721.50	$44,970.00
11		60,000	$43,171.20	$45,869.40	$48,567.60	$51,265.80	$53,964.00
12		70,000	$50,366.40	$53,514.30	$56,662.20	$59,810.10	$62,958.00
13		80,000	$57,561.60	$61,159.20	$64,756.80	$68,354.40	$71,952.00
14		90,000	$64,756.80	$68,804.10	$72,851.40	$76,898.70	$80,946.00
15		100,000	$71,952.00	$76,449.00	$80,946.00	$85,443.00	$89,940.00

Figure 2-14. *Completed two-variable data table to determine artist royalty payments*

■**Note** The initial number of units sold in cell B4 of Figures 2-13 and 2-14 and the initial artist royalty rate in cell B3 of Figure 2-14 can be any value. These values are used initially to form the worksheet function in cell B5 of Figures 2-13 and 2-14. However, the data tables substitute these initial values with the values in cells A6 through A15 in Figure 2-13, and cells B6 through B15 and cells C5 through G5 in Figure 2-14.

Now try using one-variable and two-variable data tables to calculate stock dividend payments.

Try It: Use Data Tables to Calculate Stock Dividend Payments

In this exercise, you will create one-variable and two-variable data tables to calculate stock dividend payments. These exercises are available on the Data Tables Try It Exercises.xls workbook's One-Variable Dividends Payments and Two-Variable Dividends worksheets.

Notice that on these two worksheets, cells B1 through B4 contain the initial input data, as follows:

- Cell B1 represents the price per share of stock.

- Cell B2 represents the number of shares held.

- Cell B3 represents the dividend rate per share of stock, expressed as a percentage.

- Cell B4 represents the total dividends paid, using the simple formula B1*B2*B3.

One-Variable Data Table to Calculate Stock Dividend Payments

To create the one-variable data table, start with the data on the One-Variable Dividends Payments worksheet, as shown in Figure 2-15.

Next, determine what the stock dividend payments are for shares of stock held from 25,000 to 300,000, in 25,000-share increments. Do the following to create the data table and format the results:

	A	B
1	Price Per Share	25.38
2	Shares Held	1250
3	Dividend Rate	0.0032
4	Total Dividends Paid	=B1*B2*B3

Figure 2-15. *Initial data before creating the one-variable data table to calculate stock dividend payments*

1. In cell A5, type **25000**.

2. Select cells A5 through A16.

3. Click Edit ➤ Fill ➤ Series.

4. In the Step Value box, type **25000**.

5. Click OK.

6. Select cells A4 through B16.

7. Click Data ➤ Table.

8. In the Column Input Cell box, type or click cell **B2**.

9. Click OK.

10. Select cells B5 through B16.

11. Click Format ➤ Cells.

12. Click Currency in the Category list.

13. Click OK.

Compare your results to Figure 2-16.

	A	B
1	Price Per Share	$25.38
2	Shares Held	1,250
3	Dividend Rate	0.32%
4	Total Dividends Paid	$101.52
5	25,000	$2,030.40
6	50,000	$4,060.80
7	75,000	$6,091.20
8	100,000	$8,121.60
9	125,000	$10,152.00
10	150,000	$12,182.40
11	175,000	$14,212.80
12	200,000	$16,243.20
13	225,000	$18,273.60
14	250,000	$20,304.00
15	275,000	$22,334.40
16	300,000	$24,364.80

Figure 2-16. *Completed one-variable data table to calculate stock dividend payments*

Two-Variable Data Table to Calculate Stock Dividend Payments

To create the two-variable data table, start with the data on the Two-Variable Dividends Payments worksheet. The initial data looks just like the data in the One-Variable Dividends Payments worksheet, shown earlier in Figure 2-15.

Next, determine what the stock dividend payments are for shares of stock held from 25,000 to 300,000, in 25,000-share increments and stock prices from $28.00 per share to $40.00 per share. Do the following to create the data table and format the results:

1. In cell B5, type **25000**.

2. Select cells B5 through B16.

3. Click Edit ➤ Fill ➤ Series.

4. In the Step Value box, type **25000**.

5. Click OK.

6. In cell C4, type **28**.

7. Select cells C4 through I4.

8. Click Edit ➤ Fill ➤ Series.

9. In the Step Value box, type **2**.

10. Click OK.

11. Select cells B4 through I16.

12. Click Data ➤ Table.

13. In the Row Input Cell box, type or click cell **B1**.

14. In the Column Input Cell box, type or click cell **B2**.

15. Click OK.

16. Select cells C4 through I16.

17. Click Format ➤ Cells.

18. Click Currency in the Category list.

19. Click OK.

Compare your results to Figure 2-17.

	A	B	C	D	E	F	G	H	I
1	Price Per Share	$25.38							
2	Shares Held	1,250							
3	Dividend Rate	0.32%							
4	Total Dividends Paid	$101.52	$28.00	$30.00	$32.00	$34.00	$36.00	$38.00	$40.00
5			25,000	$2,240.00	$2,400.00	$2,560.00	$2,720.00	$2,880.00	$3,040.00	$3,200.00
6			50,000	$4,480.00	$4,800.00	$5,120.00	$5,440.00	$5,760.00	$6,080.00	$6,400.00
7			75,000	$6,720.00	$7,200.00	$7,680.00	$8,160.00	$8,640.00	$9,120.00	$9,600.00
8			100,000	$8,960.00	$9,600.00	$10,240.00	$10,880.00	$11,520.00	$12,160.00	$12,800.00
9			125,000	$11,200.00	$12,000.00	$12,800.00	$13,600.00	$14,400.00	$15,200.00	$16,000.00
10			150,000	$13,440.00	$14,400.00	$15,360.00	$16,320.00	$17,280.00	$18,240.00	$19,200.00
11			175,000	$15,680.00	$16,800.00	$17,920.00	$19,040.00	$20,160.00	$21,280.00	$22,400.00
12			200,000	$17,920.00	$19,200.00	$20,480.00	$21,760.00	$23,040.00	$24,320.00	$25,600.00
13			225,000	$20,160.00	$21,600.00	$23,040.00	$24,480.00	$25,920.00	$27,360.00	$28,800.00
14			250,000	$22,400.00	$24,000.00	$25,600.00	$27,200.00	$28,800.00	$30,400.00	$32,000.00
15			275,000	$24,640.00	$26,400.00	$28,160.00	$29,920.00	$31,680.00	$33,440.00	$35,200.00
16			300,000	$26,880.00	$28,800.00	$30,720.00	$32,640.00	$34,560.00	$36,480.00	$38,400.00

Figure 2-17. *Completed two-variable data table to calculate stock dividend payments*

Troubleshooting Data Tables

When you click the Table dialog box's OK button to create a data table, one of the following error messages may appear:

This Selection Is Not Valid: This error message appears when Excel does not recognize a group of selected worksheet cells that serves as the basis of a data table. This error commonly occurs when you select a single worksheet cell or when you select a group of cells that does not form a rectangle. To fix this problem, select a group of worksheet cells that forms a rectangle at least two cells high and two cells wide, and then click Data ➤ Table again.

Input Cell Reference Is Not Valid: This error message appears when Excel does not recognize the contents of either the Row Input Cell box or the Column Input Cell box as a valid worksheet cell reference. This error message also appears when the contents of either the Row Input Cell box or the Column Input Cell box refer to more than one cell. This error commonly occurs when you incorrectly type the worksheet cell reference instead of clicking the desired cell on the worksheet. To fix this problem, type or click a single valid worksheet cell reference for the Row Input Cell box or the Column Input Cell box, and then click OK again.

Other common data table problems include the following:

- Typing or clicking a column input cell in the Row Input Cell box

- Typing or clicking a row input cell in the Column Input Cell box

- Selecting the wrong group of worksheet cells to serve as the basis of the data table, and then accidentally going ahead and creating the data table

Although Excel still creates the data table, you may not get the results that you may have expected. To re-create the data table, follow the instructions in the "Clearing Data Tables" section earlier in this chapter.

Summary

In this chapter, you learned how to create and use data tables, which can display the results of multiple formula calculations in an easy-to-use lookup table format. You also learned how to organize worksheet cell values to make it easy to create data tables by using the Table dialog box to specify a data table's row and column input cells. You practiced creating data tables by working through three Try It exercises. Finally, you learned about some common problems that may arise when you create data tables and how to fix them.

CHAPTER 3

■■■

Scenarios

A scenario is a group of Excel worksheet cell values and formulas that can be saved and swapped out automatically for another group of cell values in a worksheet. In this chapter, you will learn more about what scenarios are, when you would want to use scenarios, and how to create and work with scenarios. Then you will work through three Try It exercises to practice creating and working with scenarios on your own. The final section covers troubleshooting common problems with scenarios.

What Are Scenarios?

A *scenario* is a set of values and formulas that Excel saves as a group. You can create and save different sets of values and formulas on a worksheet as different scenarios, and then switch to any of these scenarios to view their outcomes.

For example, take the loan payment calculations shown in Figures 3-1 and 3-2. In these examples, cell B1 represents the loan's interest rate, cell B2 represents the loan term, cell B3 represents the loan amount, and cell B4 represents the loan payment. Let's call the scenario in Figure 3-1 the Three-Bedroom House scenario, and let's call the scenario in Figure 3-2 the Four-Bedroom House scenario.

	A	B
1	Interest Rate	6.90%
2	Months	360
3	Loan Amount	$200,000
4	Loan Payment	($1,317.20)

Figure 3-1. *The Three-Bedroom House loan payment calculation scenario*

	A	B
1	Interest Rate	6.30%
2	Months	360
3	Loan Amount	$250,000
4	Loan Payment	($1,547.43)

Figure 3-2. *The Four-Bedroom House loan payment calculation scenario*

By switching back and forth between these two scenarios, you can determine whether the loan payment for the four-bedroom house meets your budget constraints. Similarly, you could create and switch among additional scenarios that modify the term, the interest rate, and/or the loan amount.

In addition to switching among scenarios, with just a few mouse clicks, you can compare side-by-side scenario results in a summary report displayed as another group of worksheet cells or as a PivotTable (a special type of Excel table, designed for data analysis).

When Would I Use Scenarios?

You use scenarios to forecast the outcome of a particular set of worksheet cell values and formulas that refer to those cell values. Scenarios are particularly helpful for comparing sets of cell values to validate assumptions or analyze outcomes.

For example, Figure 3-3 shows a straight business inventory value depreciation calculation. Cell B1 represents the inventory item's initial value, cell B2 represents the inventory item's final depreciated value, cell B3 represents the number of years over which the inventory item has depreciated, and cell B4 represents the straight drop in value of the inventory item for each one of those years.

B4	▼	f_x =SLN(B1, B2, B3)	
	A	B	C
1	Initial Value	$18,000	
2	Ending Depreciated Value	$2,500	
3	Years to Depreciate	6	
4	Depreciation Per Year	$2,583.33	

Figure 3-3. *The Business Inventory Depreciation scenario*

Using this example, if you wanted to forecast the yearly depreciation over a different number of years, or raise or lower the initial value or the final depreciated value, you could define scenarios with other sets of values, and then substitute them to see the results of each scenario. This could help you decide whether to purchase a more or less expensive piece of inventory, forecast a reasonable effective life of the inventory, or forecast a possible value of the inventory at the end of its effective life.

You might be wondering why you would not use the Goal Seek feature (covered in Chapter 1) or data tables (covered in Chapter 2) instead of scenarios in the preceding example. Here are the reasons that scenarios are a better choice:

- Goal seeking would allow you to change only one of the cell values in cell B1, B2, or B3 at a time. Scenarios allow you to change any combination of cell values in these cells at once. Also, goal seeking requires you to work backward from the formula in cell B4 given an already known yearly depreciation amount. With scenarios, you work with the set values in any combination of cells B1, B2, and B3 to serve as inputs to the formula in cell B4.

- A data table would allow you to show the results of one or two of the cells B1, B2, or B3 in relation to cell B4, but with its strict two-dimensional row-and-column format, you could not show all three cells B1, B2, and B3 in relation to cell B4. With scenarios, you can see all of these cells.

In fact, scenarios allow you to substitute up to 32 changing cell values at a time. The number of scenarios stored in a worksheet is limited only by the computer's available memory. A scenario summary report can show up to 251 scenarios side by side or in a PivotTable for comparison.

How Do I Use Scenarios?

To create new scenarios or work with existing scenarios, select the worksheet containing either the existing scenarios or the cell values and formulas that you want to serve as the basis of your scenarios, and then click Tools ➤ Scenarios. You will see the Scenario Manager dialog box, as shown in Figure 3-4.

Figure 3-4. *The Scenario Manager dialog box*

The Scenario Manager dialog box contains the following controls:

- The Scenarios list displays all of the available scenarios on the selected worksheet.

- The Changing Cells box displays the cell reference for the selected scenario's changing cell values. This box is empty if there are no scenarios in the worksheet.

- The Comment box displays any comments associated with the selected scenario. This box is empty if there are no scenarios in the worksheet.

- The Show button changes the cell values associated with the selected scenario. This button is disabled if there are no scenarios in the worksheet.

- The Close button closes the Scenario Manager dialog box.

- The Add button displays the Add Scenario dialog box, so you can add a scenario.

- The Delete button deletes the selected scenario from the worksheet.

- The Edit button displays the Edit Scenario dialog box, so you can modify an existing scenario. This button is disabled if there are no scenarios in the worksheet.

- The Merge button displays the Merge Scenarios dialog box, so you can add the scenarios from one worksheet to another worksheet.

- The Summary button displays the Scenario Summary dialog box, so you can view a side-by-side summary or a PivotTable report. The Summary button is disabled if there are no scenarios in the worksheet.

The following sections describe how to create, display, edit, summarize, and merge scenarios. You will also learn how to prevent changes to scenarios.

Creating a New Scenario

To create a new scenario, click the Add button in the Scenario Manager dialog box. Excel displays the Add Scenario dialog box, as shown in Figure 3-5.

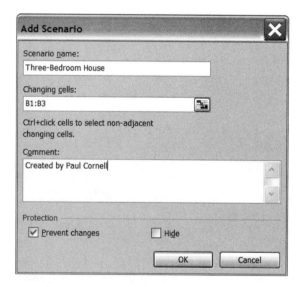

Figure 3-5. *The Add Scenario dialog box*

The Add Scenario dialog box contains the following controls:

- The Scenario Name box contains the name of the scenario.

- The Changing Cells box contains the cell reference for the changing cell values.

- The Comment box contains a comment associated with the scenario, usually the scenario's creator name and creation date. If the original scenario has been changed, typically the scenario's modifier's name and modified date will also be displayed.

- The Prevent Changes check box, when checked, prevents others from making changes to the scenario when the worksheet is protected and the Protect Sheet dialog box's Edit Scenarios check box is cleared (see the "Preventing Changes to a Scenario" section later in this chapter for details).

- The Hide check box, when checked, removes the scenario from the Scenario Manager dialog box's Scenarios list when the worksheet is protected and the Protect Sheet dialog box's Edit Scenarios check box is cleared.

When you click the OK button in the Add Scenario dialog box, Excel displays the Scenario Values dialog box, as shown in Figure 3-6. This dialog box contains one box for each changing cell reference, along with the changing cell's value.

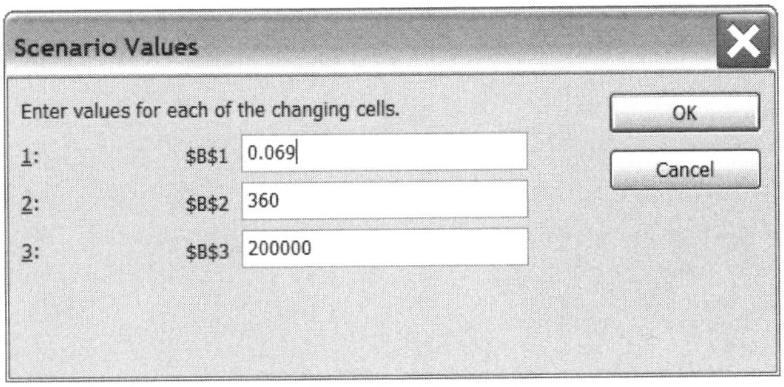

Figure 3-6. *The Scenario Values dialog box*

To add a scenario to the current worksheet, follow these steps:

1. Click Tools ➤ Scenarios.

2. In the Scenario Manager dialog box, click Add.

3. In the Scenario Name box of the Add Scenario dialog box, type a name for the scenario.

4. In the Changing Cells box, type or select the cell reference for the cells that will change.

5. Click OK.

6. In the Scenario Values dialog box, for each changing cell, type a value.

7. Click Add to create the scenario and return to the Add Scenario dialog box, or click OK to create the scenario and return to the Scenario Manager dialog box.

Displaying a Scenario

To display a scenario's results on the current worksheet, follow these steps:

1. Click Tools ➤ Scenarios.

2. In the Scenarios list, click the scenario you want to display.

3. Click Show.

Editing an Existing Scenario

To edit an existing scenario, click the Edit button in the Scenario Manager dialog box. Excel displays the Edit Scenario dialog box, which contains the same set of controls as the Add Scenario dialog box (shown earlier in Figure 3-5 and described in the previous section).

To change a scenario on the current worksheet, follow these steps:

1. Click Tools ➤ Scenarios.

2. In the Scenarios list of the Scenario Manager dialog box, click the scenario you want to change, and then click Edit.

3. In the Edit Scenario dialog box, you can change the name in the Scenario Name box, type or select the cell reference for the cells that will change in the Changing Cells box, and/or change or add a comment in the Comment box.

4. Click OK.

5. If desired, change the cell values in the Scenarios Values dialog box (see Figure 3-6, shown earlier in the chapter).

6. Click OK to save the changes and return to the Scenario Manager dialog box.

Deleting a Scenario

To remove a scenario from the current worksheet, follow these steps:

1. Click Tools ➤ Scenarios.

2. In the Scenarios list in the Scenario Manager dialog box, click the scenario you want to remove.

3. Click Delete.

Creating a Scenario Summary Report

To create a scenario summary, click the Summary button in the Scenario Manager dialog box. Excel displays the Scenario Summary dialog box, as shown in Figure 3-7.

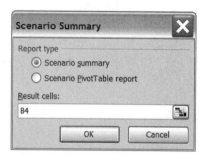

Figure 3-7. *The Scenario Summary dialog box*

The Scenario Summary dialog box contains the following controls:

- The Scenario Summary option creates a side-by-side list of changing cell values and formula results for all of the worksheet's scenarios.

- The Scenario PivotTable Report option creates a PivotTable containing the list of formula results.

- The Result Cells box displays the cell reference for the scenarios' result cells on the summary report or PivotTable.

Note To learn how to work with scenario results in a PivotTable, see "Change the layout of a PivotTable report" in Excel Help.

To display a report summarizing all of the scenario results on the current worksheet, follow these steps:

1. Click Tools ➤ Scenarios.

2. In the Scenario Manager dialog box, click Summary.

3. In the Scenario Summary dialog box, click Scenario Summary to display the side-by-side scenario results, or click Scenario PivotTable Report to display the scenario results as a PivotTable.

4. Type or click the cells containing the scenario results.

5. Click OK.

Tip You can produce scenario summary reports that are easier to read if you give each corresponding changing cell in a scenario a unique name by using the Insert ➤ Name ➤ Define command. For example, it's easier to read the summary report for a cell named Interest_Rate rather than one with the cell reference $B$1.

Merging Scenarios from Another Worksheet

To merge scenarios from another worksheet into the current worksheet, click the Merge button in the Scenario Manager dialog box. Excel displays the Merge Scenarios dialog box, as shown in Figure 3-8.

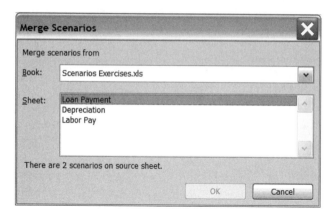

Figure 3-8. *The Merge Scenarios dialog box*

The Merge Scenarios dialog box contains the following controls:

- The Book list contains a list of all open workbooks.

- The Sheet list contains a list of all worksheets for the workbook selected in the Book list.

To add the scenarios from a worksheet in another open workbook to the current worksheet, follow these steps:

1. Click Tools ➤ Scenarios.

2. In the Scenario Manager dialog box, click Merge.

3. In the Book list of the Merge Scenarios dialog box, select the name of an open workbook.

4. In the Sheet list, select the name of the worksheet containing the scenarios you want to add to the current worksheet.

5. Click OK.

■**Caution** Merging scenarios will have unpredictable results if you merge scenarios from another worksheet that is not identical to the current worksheet. All changing cells on the worksheet containing the scenarios you want to add must refer to the corresponding changing cells on the current worksheet. The best way to avoid problems is to give each corresponding changing cell on both worksheets a unique name by using the Insert ➤ Name ➤ Define command. For example, cell B1 on Sheet1 may not necessarily contain the same value as cell B1 on Sheet2. However, if the cells were named Starting_Work_Date on both worksheets, the Starting_Work_Date cell on Sheet1 could be in cell A5, while the Starting_Work_Date on Sheet2 could be in cell B7.

Preventing Changes to a Scenario

To protect the scenarios on the current worksheet from edits, follow these steps:

1. Click Tools ➤ Scenarios.

2. In the Scenarios box of the Scenario Manager dialog box, click the scenario you want to protect, and then click Edit.

3. In the Edit Scenario dialog box, select the Prevent Changes check box to keep others from making changes to your scenarios, or select the Hide check box to prevent the scenario from appearing in the Scenarios list.

4. Click OK.

5. In the Scenario Values dialog box, click OK.

6. In the Scenario Manager dialog box, click Close.

7. To commit the protection options, click Tools ➤ Protection ➤ Protect Sheet.

8. In the Password to Unprotect Sheet box, type a password if you want to require a password to remove the protection options.

▓**Caution** If you supply a password, you should write it down and store it in a secure location. Excel cannot recover forgotten passwords.

---

9. Select the Protect Worksheet and Contents of Locked Cells check box.

10. Clear the Edit Scenarios check box.

11. Click OK.

To remove the protection options later, click Tools ➤ Protection ➤ Unprotect Sheet, type the password if one exists, and click OK.

▓**Note** Although you can create new scenarios in a protected worksheet, you cannot change or remove existing scenarios in a protected worksheet unless you clear the Edit Scenario dialog box's Prevent Changes check box. You can still change the values in a worksheet's changing cells, unless the cells themselves are locked.

Now that you know how to use the Scenario Manager dialog box, practice using it in the following Try It exercises.

Try It: Use Scenarios to Forecast Development Costs

In this exercise, you will use scenarios to forecast software development costs at a fictional software development firm. These exercises are included in the Excel workbook named Scenarios Try It Exercises.xls, which is available for download from the Source Code area of the Apress web site (http://www.apress.com). This exercise's data tables are on the workbook's Software Development worksheet.

The software development cost matrix is shown in Figure 3-9. Notice that all of the changing cells in the worksheet have been assigned names. For example, cell B10 has been assigned the name Check_1.

	A	B	C	D
1	Software Developers (SD)	9	Hourly Rate	45
2	Development Managers (DM)	=CEILING((SD/4), 1)	Hourly Rate	58
3	Project Managers (PM)	1	Hourly Rate	62.5
4				
5	Task	Hours	Resources	Subtotal
6	Write specifications	8	PM	=PM*PM_Rate*Write_Spec
7	Approve specifications	2	DM	=DM*DM_Rate*Approve_Specs
8	Write code, first milestone	80	SD, DM	=(SD*SD_Rate*Code_1)+(DM*DM_Rate*Code_1)
9	Write code, second milestone	60	SD, DM	=(SD*SD_Rate*Code_2)+(DM*DM_Rate*Code_2)
10	First checkpoint presentation	6	PM	=PM*PM_Rate*Check_1
11	Write code, third milestone	50	SD, DM	=(SD*SD_Rate*Code_3)+(DM*DM_Rate*Code_3)
12	Fix bugs, fourth milestone	40	SD, DM	=(SD*SD_Rate*Code_4)+(DM*DM_Rate*Code_4)
13	Second checkpoint presentation	6	PM	=PM*PM_Rate*Check_2
14	Release software	10	PM	=PM*PM_Rate*Release
15	Wrap-up presentation	4	SD, DM, PM	=(SD*SD_Rate*Wrap_Up)+(DM*DM_Rate*Wrap_Up)+(PM*PM_Rate*Wrap_Up)
16			Grand Total	=SUM(D6:D15)

Figure 3-9. *The software development cost matrix*

This cost matrix consists of two sections:

- Cells A1 through D3 list the number of software developers, development managers, and project managers assigned to the software development project, along with their hourly labor rates. The number of development managers is calculated in cell B2 as at least one development manager per four software developers. For example, six software developers would require two development managers.

- Cells A5 through D16 list each of the software development tasks, the number of hours required for each task, the resources required for each task, and their associated labor costs.

Worst-Case Scenario

First, create a worst-case scenario with a reduced number of resources, a higher hourly cost per resource, and a reduced number of available project hours. Do the following to create this scenario:

1. Click Tools ➤ Scenarios.

2. Click Add.

3. In the Scenario Name box, type **Worst Case Scenario**.

4. Click the Changing Cells box, and select cells B1, B3, D1 through D3, and B6 through B15. The Changing Cells box should display `B1,B3,D1:D3,B6:B15`.

5. Click OK.

6. Type the following values for each of these changing cells, pressing the Tab key after typing each value:

   SD: **3**

   PM: **1**

   SD_Rate: **60**

   DM_Rate: **70**

   PM_Rate: **75**

   Write_Spec: **2**

   Approve_Specs: **1**

   Code_1: **30**

   Code_2: **20**

   Check_1: **1**

   Code_3: **10**

   Code_4: **10**

   Check_2: **1**

   Release: **2**

   Wrap_Up: **1**

7. Click OK.

8. Click Close.

Best-Case Scenario

Next, create a best-case scenario with a large number of resources, a lower hourly cost per resource, and a large number of available project hours. Do the following to create this scenario:

1. Click Tools ➤ Scenarios.

2. Click Add.

3. In the Scenario Name box, type **Best Case Scenario**.

4. Click OK.

5. Type the following values for each of these changing cells:

SD: **15**

PM: **2**

SD_Rate: **45**

DM_Rate: **58**

PM_Rate: **62.5**

Write_Spec: **8**

Approve_Specs: **2**

Code_1: **100**

Code_2: **80**

Check_1: **10**

Code_3: **60**

Code_4: **50**

Check_2: **10**

Release: **15**

Wrap_Up: **5**

6. Click OK.

7. Click Close.

Scenario Results

Now, view each of the scenarios, first one at a time, and then side by side. Do the following to view the results:

1. Click Tools ➤ Scenarios.

2. Click Worst Case Scenario, and then click Show.

3. Click Best Case Scenario, and then click Show.

4. Click Summary.

5. Select the Scenario Summary option.

6. Click the Result Cells box, and select cells D6 through D16. The Result Cells box should display =D6:D16.

7. Click OK.

Compare your results to Figure 3-10.

		Current Values:	Worst Case Scenario	Best Case Scenario
Scenario Summary				
Changing Cells:				
SD		15	3	15
PM		2	1	2
SD_Rate		$45.00	$60.00	$45.00
DM_Rate		$58.00	$70.00	$58.00
Result Cells:				
Write_Spec_Subtotal		$1,000.00	$150.00	$1,000.00
Approve_Specs_Subtotal		$464.00	$70.00	$464.00
Code_1_Subtotal		$90,700.00	$7,500.00	$90,700.00
Code_2_Subtotal		$72,560.00	$5,000.00	$72,560.00
Check_1_Subtotal		$1,250.00	$75.00	$1,250.00
Code_3_Subtotal		$54,420.00	$2,500.00	$54,420.00
Code_4_Subtotal		$45,350.00	$2,500.00	$45,350.00
Check_2_Subtotal		$1,250.00	$75.00	$1,250.00
Release_Subtotal		$1,875.00	$150.00	$1,875.00
Wrap_Up_Subtotal		$5,160.00	$325.00	$5,160.00
Grand_Total		$274,029.00	$18,345.00	$274,029.00

Figure 3-10. *The software development scenario summary report (panes split for readability)*

Try It: Use Scenarios to Forecast Sales

In this exercise, you will use scenarios to forecast soft drink sales for an independent soft drink bottler. These exercises are available on the Scenarios Try It Exercises.xls workbook's Soft Drink Sales worksheet.

The soft drink sales forecast matrix is shown in Figure 3-11. Notice that all of the changing cells in the worksheet have been assigned names. For example, cell C5 has the name N_GSales.

	A	B	C	D
1	Case Suggested Retail Price	27.99		
2	Case Wholesale Discount	0.17		
3				
4	Region	Cases Sold	Gross Sales	Net Sales
5	North	35000	=MSRP*N_Sold	=(MSRP*(1-Discount))*N_Sold
6	East	30000	=MSRP*E_Sold	=(MSRP*(1-Discount))*E_Sold
7	South	20000	=MSRP*S_Sold	=(MSRP*(1-Discount))*S_Sold
8	West	43000	=MSRP*W_Sold	=(MSRP*(1-Discount))*W_Sold
9	Totals	=SUM(B5:B8)	=SUM(C5:C8)	=SUM(D5:D8)

Figure 3-11. *The soft drink sales forecast matrix*

This sales forecast matrix consists of two sections:

- Cells A1 and B2 list the suggested retail price per case of soft drinks, as well as the wholesale discount per case.

- Cells A4 through D9 list each sales region, the number of cases sold per region, the gross sales proceeds per region, and the net sales proceeds per region.

Summer Scenario

First, create a scenario that forecasts the number of cases sold in the summer. Do the following to create this scenario:

1. Click Tools ➤ Scenarios.

2. Click Add.

3. In the Scenario Name box, type **Summer Scenario**.

4. Click the Changing Cells box, and select cells B1, B2, and B5 through B8. The Changing Cells box should display B1:B2,B5:B8.

5. Click OK.

6. Type the following values for each of these changing cells:

    MSRP: **29.99**

    Discount: **0.15**

    N_Sold: **45000**

    E_Sold: **52000**

    S_Sold: **58000**

    W_Sold: **42000**

7. Click OK.

8. Click Close.

Winter Scenario

Next, create a scenario that forecasts the number of cases sold in the winter. Do the following to create this scenario:

1. Click Tools ➤ Scenarios.

2. Click Add.

3. In the Scenario Name box, type **Winter Scenario**.

4. Click OK.

5. Type the following values for each of these changing cells:

   MSRP: **24.99**

   Discount: **0.17**

   N_Sold: **29000**

   E_Sold: **33250**

   S_Sold: **38000**

   W_Sold: **26500**

6. Click OK.

7. Click Close.

Scenario Results

Now, view each of the scenarios, first one at a time, and then in a PivotTable. Do the following to view the results:

1. Click Tools ➤ Scenarios.

2. Click Summer Scenario, and then click Show.

3. Click Winter Scenario, and then click Show.

4. Click Summary.

5. Select the Scenario PivotTable Report option.

6. Click the Result Cells box, and select cells C5 through D9. The Result Cells box should display C5:D9.

7. Click OK.

Compare your results to Figure 3-12.

	A	B	C	D	I	J	K
1	$B$1:$B$2,$B$5:$B$8 by	(All) ▾					
2							
3		Result Cells ▾					
4	$B$1:$B$2,$B$5:$B$8 ▾	N_GSales	N_NSales	E_GSales	W_NSales	Gross_Sales	Net_Sales
5	Original Values	979650	813109.5	839700	998963.1	3582720	2973657.6
6	Summer Scenario	1349550	1147117.5	1559480	1070643	5908030	5021825.5
7	Winter Scenario	724710	601509.3	830917.5	549655.05	3167482.5	2629010.475

Figure 3-12. *The soft drink sales forecast scenario summary PivotTable (panes split for readability)*

Try It: Use Scenarios to Forecast Rental Volumes

In this exercise, you will use scenarios to forecast video rental sales for a national video rental store chain. These exercises are available on the Scenarios Try It Exercises.xls workbook's Video Rentals worksheet.

The video rental forecast matrix is shown in Figure 3-13. Notice that all of the changing cells in the worksheet have been assigned names. For example, cell B7 has the name Thursday_Factor.

	A	B	C	D	J
1	Base Average Daily Video Rentals Volume	200			
2		Day Weighting Factor			
3	Sunday	0.8			
4	Monday	0.5			
5	Tuesday	1			
6	Wednesday	0.6			
7	Thursday	0.7			
8	Friday	1.1			
9	Saturday	0.9			
10					
11					
12	City	Rental Stores	Sunday	Monday	Subtotals
13	Seattle	4	=Base_Volume*Sunday_Factor*Seattle_Stores	=Base_Volume*Monday_Factor*Seattle_Stores	=SUM(C13:I13)
14	Kirkland	3	=Base_Volume*Sunday_Factor*Kirkland_Stores	=Base_Volume*Monday_Factor*Kirkland_Stores	=SUM(C14:I14)
15	Redmond	2	=Base_Volume*Sunday_Factor*Redmond_Stores	=Base_Volume*Monday_Factor*Redmond_Stores	=SUM(C15:I15)
16	Woodinville	1	=Base_Volume*Sunday_Factor*Woodinville_Stores	=Base_Volume*Monday_Factor*Woodinville_Stores	=SUM(C16:I16)
17		Subtotals	=SUM(C13:C16)	=SUM(D13:D16)	=SUM(J13:J16)

Figure 3-13. *The video rental forecast matrix (panes split for readability)*

This rental forecast matrix consists of three sections:

- Cell A1 lists the base average video rentals volume per day.

- Cells A2 through B9 provide a way to adjust the base average daily video rentals volume to account for fluctuations in business by day of the week. For example, a factor of 1.1 means that stores expect to do 110% of their base average daily video rentals volume on that day.

- Cells A12 through J17 list the cities with rental stores, the number of rental stores in each city, and total number of forecast video rentals per day.

Blockbuster Week Scenario

First, create a scenario that forecasts the number of video rentals during a blockbuster week. Do the following to create this scenario:

1. Click Tools ➤ Scenarios.

2. Click Add.

3. In the Scenario Name box, type **Blockbuster Week Scenario**.

4. Click the Changing Cells box, and select cells B1, B3 through B9, and B13 through B16. The Changing Cells box should display `B1,B3:B9,B13:B16`.

5. Click OK.

6. Type the following values for each of these changing cells:

> Base_Volume: **300**
>
> Sunday_Factor: **1.0**
>
> Monday_Factor: **0.7**
>
> Tuesday_Factor: **1.6**
>
> Wednesday_Factor: **0.9**
>
> Thursday_Factor: **1.0**
>
> Friday_Factor: **1.3**
>
> Saturday_Factor: **1.2**
>
> Seattle_Stores: **4**
>
> Kirkland_Stores: **3**
>
> Redmond_Stores: **2**
>
> Woodinville_Stores: **1**

7. Click OK.

8. Click Close.

Regular Week Scenario

Next, create a scenario that forecasts the number of video rentals during a regular week. Do the following to create this scenario:

1. Click Tools ➤ Scenarios.

2. Click Add.

3. In the Scenario Name box, type **Non-Blockbuster Week Scenario**.

4. Click OK.

5. Type the following values for each of these changing cells:

> Base_Volume: **200**
>
> Sunday_Factor: **0.8**
>
> Monday_Factor: **0.5**
>
> Tuesday_Factor: **1.0**
>
> Wednesday_Factor: **0.6**
>
> Thursday_Factor: **0.7**
>
> Friday_Factor: **1.1**
>
> Saturday_Factor: **0.9**
>
> Seattle_Stores: **4**
>
> Kirkland_Stores: **3**
>
> Redmond_Stores: **2**
>
> Woodinville_Stores: **1**

6. Click OK.

7. Click Close.

Scenario Results

Now, view each of the scenarios, first one at a time, and then side by side. Do the following to view the results:

1. Click Tools ➤ Scenarios.

2. Click Blockbuster Week Scenario, and then click Show.

3. Click Non-Blockbuster Week Scenario, and then click Show.

4. Click Summary.

5. Select the Scenario Summary option.

6. Click the Result Cells box, and select cells C17 through J17. The Result Cells box should display C17:J17.

7. Click OK.

Compare your results to Figure 3-14.

B	C	D	F	G
Scenario Summary		Current Values:	Blockbuster Week Scenario	Non-Blockbuster Week Scenario
Changing Cells:				
	Base_Volume	200	300	200
	Sunday_Factor	0.8	1	0.8
	Monday_Factor	0.5	0.7	0.5
	Tuesday_Factor	1	1.6	1
	Woodinville_Stores	1	1	1
Result Cells:				
	Sunday_Subtotal	1,600	3,000	1,600
	Monday_Subtotal	1,000	2,100	1,000
	Tuesday_Subtotal	2,000	4,800	2,000
	Wednesday_Subtotal	1,200	2,700	1,200
	Thursday_Subtotal	1,400	3,000	1,400
	Friday_Subtotal	2,200	3,900	2,200
	Saturday_Subtotal	1,800	3,600	1,800
	Grand_Rentals_Total	11,200	23,100	11,200

Figure 3-14. *The video rental forecast scenario summary report (panes split for readability)*

Troubleshooting Scenarios

When you add or edit a scenario, one of the following messages may appear:

At Least One of the Changing Cells You Specified Contains a Formula: This message may appear when you type or select one or more cell references to one or more formulas in the Add Scenario or Edit Scenario dialog box's Changing Cells box. In this case, the formulas in the changing cells will be replaced by constant values when you show a scenario. To prevent this from happening, click OK, and then click Cancel. Then create or edit the scenario again.

Scenario names must be unique: This message may appear after you create a scenario and type a scenario name in the Scenario Name box, even though no scenarios appear in the Scenario Manager dialog box. This message appears when the worksheet is protected and a scenario already exists in the worksheet with the same name as the name you typed in the Scenario Name box. To resolve this issue, type a different name in the Scenario Name box, or unprotect the worksheet and delete the scenario with the conflicting name.

Also note the following restrictions on scenarios:

- You cannot undo deleting a scenario. If you want to retrieve the scenario, you must re-create it.

- You cannot undo running a scenario. If you want to revert back to the original values, you must manually type them in, or you must have already created a scenario containing the original values. If you accidentally run a scenario that replaces a cell containing a formula with a value, there is no way to revert the cell's contents back to the formula. Unfortunately, you must re-create the formula.

Summary

In this chapter, you learned about scenarios, which are groups of Excel worksheet cell values and formulas that can be saved and exchanged with other groups of cell values in a worksheet. You learned how to work with scenarios on worksheets by using the Scenario Manager dialog box. You also worked through three Try It exercises to practice creating scenarios and viewing their results. Finally, you learned about some messages you might see when creating or editing scenarios, as well as some restrictions on scenarios.

CHAPTER 4

■■■

Solver

Solver helps you find a single worksheet cell formula's desired exact value, minimum possible value, or maximum possible value. Solver does this by changing the worksheet cell values you specify to produce the selected cell formula's desired value. You can also apply restrictions to the cell values that Solver can use to find the desired value.

In this chapter, you will learn more about what Solver is, when you would want to use Solver, and how to work with Solver. Then you will work through three basic Try It exercises, as well as seven more involved exercises, to practice using Solver on your own. The final section in this chapter describes how to troubleshoot common problems with using Solver.

What Is Solver?

In its simplest terms, Solver is a tool that obtains a certain value, a maximum value, or a minimum value of one worksheet cell by changing other related cells. Solver will change the worksheet cell value you specify to the specified value, highest value, or lowest value for a worksheet cell formula. For example, you can change a business's forecasted budget amount and see the effect on the projected business's profit.

You can also restrict the allowed values that Solver can use. For instance, you can specify that a manufacturing plant cannot operate for more than 24 hours in a single workday.

For another example, consider the problem of determining the best theater ticket prices and number of tickets to sell at those prices for a theater to achieve a desired box office income amount. In Chapter 1, you saw how to use Excel's Goal Seek feature to solve this problem. As you may recall, the Theater Ticket Prices worksheet lists three ticket price points for child, adult, and senior tickets, as shown in Figure 4-1. The target box office income is simply the sum of the child, adult, and senior ticket prices multiplied by their respective number of tickets to sell.

	A	B	C	D	
1		Price Per Ticket	Tickets to Sell		
2	Child Ticket	$3.00	100		
3	Adult Ticket	$5.00	60		
4	Senior Ticket	$4.00	100		
5					
6	Box Office Income	$1,000.00	← (B2*C2)+(B3*C3)+(B4*C4)		

Figure 4-1. *Forecasting optimal theater ticket prices*

As you saw in Chapter 1, using Goal Seek, you can look for one value at a time: the number of tickets sold for child, adult, or senior, or the ticket prices for child, adult, or senior. With Solver, you can still solve for only one value at a time, but you gain the flexibility of solving for specific values, minimum values, and maximum values, and applying various other constraints.

For instance, you can use Solver to figure out how many tickets to sell to achieve an income of exactly $1,000.00, subject to the following constraints:

- Child tickets sell only for $3.00 each.

- Adult tickets sell only for $5.00 each.

- Senior tickets sell only for $4.00 each.

- No more than 100 tickets can be sold to children, adults, or seniors.

- Only full tickets can be sold (no fractional ticket sales are allowed).

You can run Solver to produce the following result: If you sell 100 child tickets, 60 adult tickets, and 100 senior tickets at their respective ticket prices, you will receive $1,000.00.

In this case, Solver can suggest other possible combinations of ticket sales to solve this problem. For example, you could sell 96 child tickets, 92 adult tickets, and 63 senior tickets; or you could sell 60 child tickets, 92 adult tickets, and 90 senior tickets; and so on. As you will learn in this chapter, some Solver problems have no optimal solution, some problems have only one possible solution, and others have multiple possible solutions.

As another example of applying a constraint, take the recipe calculations for making a batch of cupcakes, as shown in Figure 4-2. Let's say there is the constraint of having only a dozen eggs in stock (cell B5). Using Solver, you can try to find the maximum number of cupcakes that can be produced. In this case, Solver finds the answer in cell B12: 96 cupcakes.

	A	B	C
1	Cupcakes/24 →	4	cake mix (packages)
2	(Cupcakes/24)*1.25 →	5	water (cups)
3	(Cupcakes/24)*0.33 →	1.32	vegetable oil (cups)
4	Cupcakes/24 →	4	orange-flavored gelatin (boxes)
5	(Cupcakes/24)*3 →	12	egg whites
6	(Cupcakes/24)*3 →	12	powdered sugar (cups)
7	(Cupcakes/24)*0.33 →	1.32	butter (cups)
8	Cupcakes/24 →	4	vanilla (teaspoons)
9	(Cupcakes/24)*2 →	8	milk (teaspoons)
10	(Cupcakes/24)*0.33 →	1.32	white baking chips (cups)
11			
12	Cupcakes →	96	cupcakes (yield)

Figure 4-2. *Estimating baking recipe yield using limited food resources*

When Would I Use Solver?

You can use Solver to help find an optimal solution to a problem: an exact specified outcome, the lowest possible outcome, or the highest possible outcome. Typical Solver applications in business include financial, budgeting, and investment problems, as well as resource management problems (consisting of resources such as people, equipment, materials, or time). Solver is also widely used in the academic community to solve mathematical equations and run scientific simulations.

The Goal Seek feature is initially easier to learn and use than Solver. However, learning about Solver is worth the time investment, as it is more powerful than Goal Seek. While both Goal Seek and Solver are designed to solve a problem in conjunction with a single target cell, Solver has the following advantages:

- Goal Seek can work with only a single changing cell, while Solver can tackle problems involving several changing cells. In fact, Solver can work with up to 200 changing cells.

- Solver can try to find the highest or lowest possible values, as well as exact specified values.

- Solver allows you to specify restrictions, or constraints, for cell values. For example, you can specify that certain cell values must be equal to, higher than, or lower than a given number. In fact, you can specify up to 500 constraints in a Solver problem, consisting of up to two constraints with up to 200 changing cells per constraint, plus 100 additional constraints. (Actually, when the Solver Options dialog box's Assume Linear Model check box is selected, there is theoretically no limit to the number of constraints.)

- Goal Seek settings are not saved when you close a workbook. However, the last Solver settings you make for each worksheet are retained. You can also save multiple Solver settings (called *models*), and then load them later instead of entering all of the Solver settings each time you want to run a Solver problem.

■**Note** One advantage to using Goal Seek over Solver is that while Goal Seek can reference a changing cell and a cell containing a formula on different worksheets, Solver can work with changing cells only on the same worksheet as the target formula's cell.

You will learn how to work with each of these aspects of Solver in the following sections.

How Do I Use Solver?

As you learn more about Solver, you will encounter some terms that may be new to you. To help you understand the following basic Solver terminology, refer to Figure 4-3, which shows bug counts for a software development project.

- The *target cell* is the cell that you want Solver to set to a maximum, minimum, or specified value. In Figure 4-3, any single cell in the cell range B6 through F7 and G2 through H7 is eligible to be selected as a target cell.

- The *objective* is the desired goal or outcome of the problem that you want Solver to reach. The target cell represents Solver's problem-solving goal. In Figure 4-3, you might be interested in selecting cell G7 as the target cell to have the value 25 after running Solver.

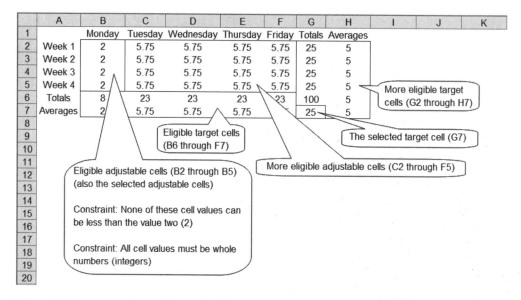

Figure 4-3. *Bug counts for a software development project before running Solver*

- The *adjustable cells* (also referred to as *changing cells*) are the cells that Solver will change (adjust the values of) to achieve the desired objective. In Figure 4-3, the eligible adjustable cells are B2 through F5. In Figure 4-3, you could choose all of the eligible adjustable cells.

- The *constraints* are the problem's restrictions that you place on the adjustable cells. Solver must adhere to these constraints as it tries to change the adjustable cells to meet the objective. In Figure 4-3, you could create two possible constraints. First, you could constrain the problem so that none of the adjustable cells' (cells B2 through F5) values can be less than 2. Second, you could require all of the adjustable cells' (again, cells B2 through B5) values to be whole numbers (integers).

- A *model* is the set of target cell, all adjustable cells, and any constraints for the current problem that you want Solver to solve.

When you run Solver using the model as it is defined in this section, Solver produces the results shown in Figure 4-4.

	A	B	C	D	E	F	G	H
1		Monday	Tuesday	Wednesday	Thursday	Friday	Totals	Averages
2	Week 1	2	5.75	5.75	5.75	5.75	25	5
3	Week 2	2	5.75	5.75	5.75	5.75	25	5
4	Week 3	2	5.75	5.75	5.75	5.75	25	5
5	Week 4	2	5.75	5.75	5.75	5.75	25	5
6	Totals	8	23	23	23	23	100	5
7	Averages	2	5.75	5.75	5.75	5.75	25	5

Figure 4-4. *Solver reaches the objective for the current model. Cell G7 contains the value 25, and the values in cells B2 through B5 are greater than or equal to 2 and are integers (whole numbers).*

Installing Solver

Since Solver may not always be available when Excel is installed, you should confirm that Solver is available before you try to use it. If the Solver command doesn't appear on the Tools menu, click Tools ➤ Add-Ins, select the Solver Add-In check box, and click OK. Then Solver should be listed on the Tools menu.

If the Solver Add-In check box is not visible in the Add-Ins Available list, you must install Solver by running the Microsoft Office Setup program again and selecting Solver from the list of available Excel add-ins. Then when you restart Excel, Solver should appear on the Tools menu.

Setting Solver Parameters

To use Solver, click Tools ➤ Solver. The Solver Parameters dialog box appears, as shown in Figure 4-5.

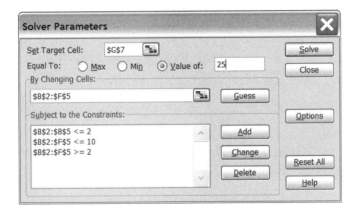

Figure 4-5. *The Solver Parameters dialog box*

The Solver Parameters dialog box contains the following controls, from top to bottom and left to right:

- The Set Target Cell box contains a reference to a single worksheet cell that you want to set to a maximum, minimum, or specific value. The cell referenced in this box must contain a formula.

- The Equal To options specify whether you want the cell referenced in the Set Target Cell box to be maximized, minimized, or set to a certain value.

  - The Max option attempts to reach the highest target cell value subject to any specified constraints.

  - The Min option attempts to reach the lowest target cell value subject to any specified constraints.

  - The Value Of option attempts to reach a specific value subject to any specified constraints. If you click the Value Of option, type the specific value in the Value Of box to the right of the Value Of option. The default value is 0 (zero).

- The By Changing Cells box contains a reference to the worksheet cells that you want Solver to try to adjust until the cell referenced in the Set Target Cell box reaches its specified maximum, minimum, or exact value, subject to any specified constraints. For Solver to work properly, the cells referenced in the By Changing Cells box must be somehow related to the cell referenced in the Set Target Cell box.

- The Guess button asks Solver to try to guess all nonformula cells related to the Set Target Cell box's referenced worksheet cell formula and place those nonformula cell references in the By Changing Cells box.

- The Subject to the Constraints list displays the current restrictions for the problem.

- The Add button displays the Add Constraint dialog box, so you can add a constraint to the problem.

- The Change button displays the Change Constraint dialog box, so you can modify a constraint.

- The Delete button removes the constraint selected in the Subject to the Constraints list.

- The Solve button tells Solver to start finding a solution for the specified problem.

- The Close button closes the Solver Parameters dialog box without solving the specified problem.

■**Note** When you click the Close button, Solver retains any changes you made to the Solver Parameters dialog box on the current worksheet by using the Options, Add, Change, and Delete buttons. The next time you click Tools ➤ Solver on the current worksheet, those retained changes will reappear.

- The Options button displays the Solver Options dialog box, so you can specify Solver settings and advanced Solver options.

- The Reset All button clears all of the settings in the Solver Parameters dialog box and resets all of the settings in the Solver Options dialog box to their default values.

- The Help button displays an Excel Help topic that describes how to use the dialog box. (As you would expect, this applies to the Help button in each of Solver's dialog boxes.)

To set Solver parameters, follow these steps:

1. Click Tools ➤ Solver.

2. If you want to clear the current settings for Solver parameters and options, click Reset All, and then click OK.

3. Click the Set Target cell box, and click or type a single cell reference.

4. Click the Max, Min, or Value Of radio button. If you chose Value Of, type a value in the Value Of text box.

5. Click the By Changing Cells box, and click or type a reference to the worksheet cells that you want Solver to try to adjust.

6. If you want to add constraints, click Add, and then specify constraints, as described in the next section.

7. Click Solve.

8. Click OK.

The following sections describe how to add and change constraints, set Solver options, and work with Solver models. You will also learn how to work with Solver results, trial solutions, and reports.

Adding and Changing Constraints

When you click the Solver Parameters dialog box's Add button, the Add Constraint dialog box appears, as shown in Figure 4-6.

Figure 4-6. *The Add Constraint dialog box*

To add a constraint, follow these steps:

1. In the Cell Reference box, type or select the cell references for which you want to restrict values.

2. In the operator list between the Cell Reference and Constraint boxes, click the relationship that you want between the referenced cells and the constraint. The relationship choices are as follows:

   - The <= item specifies that the referenced cell values must be less than or equal to the constraint.

   - The = item specifies that the referenced cell values must be equal to the constraint.

   - The >= item specifies that the referenced cell values must be greater than or equal to the constraint.

   - The Int item specifies that the referenced cell values must be integers. If you click Int in the operator list, Integer appears in the Constraint box. You can apply the Int relationship only to constraints on adjustable cells.

- The Bin item specifies that the referenced cell values must be only one of two values, such as Yes/No, True/False, or 0/1. If you click Bin in the operator list, Binary appears in the Constraint box. You can apply the Bin relationship only to constraints on adjustable cells.

■**Caution** Adding Int (integer) constraints to a Solver problem can significantly increase a problem's complexity, resulting in lengthy delays and possibly even prematurely stopping Solver before it can find a solution.

---

3. In the Constraint box, type a number, a cell reference, or a formula (if you selected an operator other than Int or Bin).

4. Click the OK button to accept the constraint and return to the Solver Parameters dialog box, or click the Add button to accept the constraint and prepare to add another constraint without returning to the Solver Parameters dialog box first. You can also click the Cancel button to cancel the constraint entry and return to the Solver Parameters dialog box.

To change an existing constraint, click the Solver Parameters dialog box's Change button. The Change Constraint dialog box appears. This dialog box looks identical to the Add Constraint dialog box. Here, you can modify the cell reference, operator, and/or constraint value, using the same procedure as described in the previous steps for adding a constraint.

Setting Solver Options

When you click the Solver Parameters dialog box's Options button, the Solver Options dialog box appears, as shown in Figure 4-7.

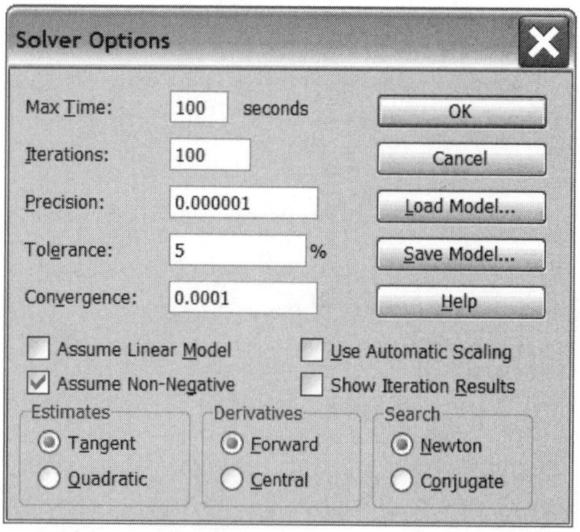

Figure 4-7. *The Solver Options dialog box*

The Solver Options dialog box contains the following settings:

Max Time: This box specifies the number of seconds that you want to allow Solver to try to reach your solution's objective. Although you can enter a value as high as 32,767 seconds (that's over nine hours!), the default value of 100 seconds (just over a minute and a half) is adequate for most small problems. If Solver has not yet found a solution after the time period in the Max Time box is reached, Solver pauses and displays the Show Trial Solution dialog box to give you the option of stopping without an optimal solution or continuing for another equal time period.

Iterations: This box specifies the maximum number of calculations that you want to allow Solver to try before it reaches your solution's objective or gives up. As with the Max Time box, while you can enter a value as high as 32,767 iterations, the default value of 100 iterations is adequate for most small problems. If Solver cannot reach the objective after the number of tries in the Iterations box, Solver stops and displays the Show Trial Solution dialog box to give you the option of stopping without an optimal solution or continuing for another equal set of iterations.

Precision: This box specifies to what level of exactness the value of a constraint cell meets a target value or satisfies a lower or upper bound. The Precision value must be a fractional number between 0 and 1. The smaller the number in the Precision box (the higher the number of decimal places), the higher the degree of precision. For example, 0.000001 is a higher precision than 0.01. Solver continues trying to reach the problem's objective until the constraints are obtained within this degree of precision. For example, if the value in this box is 0.000001, and some constraint states that a cell value must equal 19, Solver will stop when the cell's value is within 0.000001 of 19; that is, between 18.999999 and 19.000001.

Tolerance: This box specifies the percentage by which the target cell of a problem with integer constraints can differ from the true optimal value and still have Solver consider it an acceptable solution to the problem. A higher tolerance tends to speed up Solver's time to find a solution. Solver will stop when the target cell's value is within this percent of the constraint value. The default tolerance is 5%.

Convergence: This box specifies the amount of relative change you want to allow Solver in its last five calculations before Solver stops with a solution. Solver uses the value in the Convergence box to determine when a proposed solution is significantly better than the previous proposed solution. If the change in the two proposed solutions is less than or equal to the value in the Convergence box, Solver will stop and declare that it has found a solution. Convergence applies only to nonlinear problems and must be indicated by a fractional number between 0 and 1. The smaller the number in the Convergence box, the smaller the convergence. For example, 0.0001 (the default value) is less relative change, and a smaller convergence, than 0.01. However, the smaller the number in the Convergence box, the more time it takes for Solver to reach a solution.

Assume Linear Model: This check box speeds up Solver's solution process. Check it if you know that your problem can be solved with linear functions. A *linear function* is a function that can be written as the sum of a series of variables, where each variable is multiplied by some constant value. A *nonlinear function* involves using some mathematical operation other than summation. Solver sometimes struggles with arriving at a solution to nonlinear problems, because it is not always possible beforehand for Solver to determine which is the best approach to take. If a Solver problem is linear and you select the Assume Linear Model check box, Solver uses a very efficient algorithm (the *simplex method*) to find the model's solution. If a Solver model is linear and you do not select the Assume Linear Model check box, Solver uses an inefficient algorithm (the *GRG2 method*), and it might have difficulty finding the model's solution.

Assume Non-Negative: This check box tells Solver to assume a lower limit of zero for all adjustable cells for which you have not set lower-limit constraints.

Use Automatic Scaling: This check box applies scaling automatically. Check it when problem input and output values have large differences in order of magnitude; for example, when maximizing the percentage of profit based on billion dollar cash flows. Poorly scaled models (models where the typical values of the problem's objective and its constraints differ by several orders of magnitude) are one of the most common reasons why Solver appears to stop early without reaching a true optimal solution. Therefore, it is a good idea to select the Use Automatic Scaling box if you think you're working with a poorly scaled model.

Show Iteration Results: This check box has Solver pause, display the Show Trial Solution dialog box, and show its interim results, for each calculation of the current problem.

Estimates: This area specifies the approach used to obtain initial estimates of the basic variables in each one-dimensional search.

- Choose the Tangent option if you know you have a linear problem to solve. The Tangent option instructs Solver to use an algorithm that performs a linear extrapolation from a tangent vector, and therefore favors linear problems. Clicking the Tangent option is faster, but less accurate, than clicking the Quadratic option.

- Select the Quadratic option if you know you have a nonlinear problem to solve. The Quadratic option instructs Solver to use an algorithm that performs a quadratic extrapolation, which can greatly improve the results on highly nonlinear problems.

Derivatives: This area specifies the algorithm that Solver uses to begin calculating possible solutions by estimating partial derivatives of the problem's objective and its constraints.

- Select the Forward option for most problems, especially those problems in which the constraint values change relatively slowly.

- Choose the Central option for those problems in which you know that the constraints may change rapidly, especially near their limits.

▓**Tip** Although clicking the Central option forces Solver to make more calculations, it might be useful to choose this option if Solver ever displays a message stating that a solution could not be improved.

Search: This area specifies the algorithm that Solver uses to determine the next direction it will search for a possible solution after each of its calculations.

- Select the Newton option to use a quasi-Newton algorithm that results in a highly accurate search for possible solutions.

- Choose the Conjugate option to use a less accurate search when you have a large problem that consumes a lot of computing resources, or when using Solver to step through iterations reveals very slow progress.

After you've specified Solver options, you can click one of the buttons along the right side of the dialog box:

- Click the OK button to apply the selected Solver options and return to the Solver Parameters dialog box.

- Click the Cancel button to disregard any changes to the current Solver options and return to the Solver Parameters dialog box.

- Click the Load Model button to display the Load Model dialog box, where you can specify the cell references for the model that you want to load. Working with Solver models is covered in the next section.

- Click the Save Model button to display the Save Model dialog box, where you can specify where to save the current model. You need to click this button only when you want to save more than one model with a worksheet, as Solver automatically saves the first model in the current worksheet.

Saving and Loading Solver Models

A Solver *model* is the set of target cell, all adjustable cells, and any constraints for the current problem that you want Solver to solve. Instead of entering a model's target cell, adjustable cells, and constraints every time you open the Solver Parameters dialog box, you can save time by loading an existing model and then running Solver. You can also save your own models that you can load into Solver later.

▪**Note** You can also save the last selections in the Solver Parameters dialog box within a worksheet by simply clicking File ➤ Save.

Saving a Solver Model

To save an existing model, do the following:

1. Run Solver to solve the problem that you want to save.

2. Click Tools ➤ Solver.

3. Click Options.

4. Click Save Model.

5. Select or type the address for the first cell of a vertical range of empty cells in which you want to place the problem model.

6. Click OK.

Tip It is advisable to save a model in a blank area below the last row of data on a worksheet, because for larger problems, the range of cells that describe the model can grow quite long. Additional models can be saved in other blank areas of the worksheet, as long as each range of cells that describes a model does not overlap with other cell ranges describing other models.

If you want to store a workbook's models in a central location, in step 5 of the preceding procedure, you can save all worksheets models on a single worksheet separate from the worksheets containing the target and changing cells. If you do store a worksheet model on a workbook separate from the originating worksheet, you may want to add a brief note or comment about this near the stored model for future reference.

Solver stores the model's target cell, adjustable cells, constraints, and other option settings in a vertical column of cells, beginning with the cell specified in the Save Model dialog box. For example, look at the model stored in the worksheet shown in Figure 4-8.

14	=MAX($B$12)
15	=COUNT($B$12)
16	=$B$5<=12
17	={100,100,0.000001,0.05,TRUE,FALSE,FALSE,1,1,1,0.0001,FALSE}

Figure 4-8. *A Solver model's description*

The cells in this problem can be interpreted as follows (in this order):

- Cell 14 instructs Solver to try to find the maximum value for cell B12.

- Cell 15 instructs Solver to change only cell B12.

- Cell 16 imposes a constraint that cell B5 cannot exceed the value 12.

- Cell 17 lists the settings in the Solver Options dialog box, in the following order:

  - A Max Time setting of 100 seconds

  - An Iterations setting of 100

  - A Precision setting of 0.000001

  - A Tolerance setting of 0.05 (5%)

  - The Assume Linear Model check box selected (TRUE)

  - The Assume Non-Negative check box unselected (FALSE)

- The Use Automatic Scaling check box unselected (FALSE)

- The Tangent option selected (1)

- The Forward option selected (1)

- The Newton option selected (1)

- A Convergence setting of 0.0001

- The Show Iteration Results check box unselected (FALSE)

▓**Note** If the Quadratic, Central, and Conjugate options were selected, you would see the settings 2, 2, 2 instead of 1, 1, 1. If the Tangent, Central, and Newton options were selected, you would see the settings 1, 2, 1, and so on.

Loading a Solver Model

To load a Solver model, you must have previously saved that model somewhere in the workbook. To load and run a saved Solver model, do the following:

1. Click Tools ➤ Solver.

2. Click Options.

3. Click Load Model.

4. Click or type the reference for the entire range of cells that contains the desired problem model. For example, in Figure 4-8, the model is defined in the range of cells 14 through 17.

5. Click OK two times to return to the Solver Parameters dialog box.

6. Click Solve.

▓**Caution** You must select all of the cells that define the desired problem model when you attempt to load the model. Otherwise, only the settings in the selected cells will be transferred to the Solver Parameters and Solver Options dialog boxes, which will leave the other controls in the Solver Parameters and Solver Options dialog boxes in an unpredictable state when you run Solver.

Working with the Solver Results

When Solver stops (because it found a solution, it could not find a feasible solution, the user stopped it, or for some other reason), a completion message appears in the Solver Results dialog box, as shown in Figure 4-9.

Tip You can interrupt Solver as it is trying to solve a problem by pressing the Esc key. Excel will then recalculate the worksheet with the last values that were found for the model's adjustable cells.

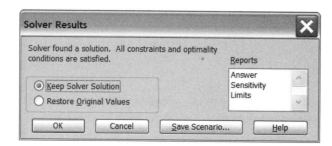

Figure 4-9. *The Solver Results dialog box*

The Solver Results dialog box will display one of the following results messages when it has found a solution:

Solver Found a Solution. All Constraints and Optimality Conditions Are Satisfied: This message is displayed when Solver finds a solution within the model's constraints and the Solver Options dialog box's precision setting, and when appropriate, Solver finds the target cell's maximum or minimum value.

Solver Has Converged to the Current Solution. All Constraints Are Satisfied: This message is displayed when the relative change in the model's target cell is less than the Solver Options dialog box's Convergence setting for the last five trial calculations.

Tip If you provide a smaller value for the Convergence setting, Solver could try for a better solution; however, providing a smaller Convergence setting would take more solution time.

To interpret other Solver Results dialog box messages, see the "Solver Dialog Box Error Messages" section later in this chapter.

In the Solver Results dialog box, you can choose the Keep Solver Solution option to accept Solver's proposed solution and place the resulting values into the adjustable cells. Alternatively, click the Restore Original Values option to restore the original values in the model's adjustable cells.

You can also use the Reports list to create the type of report you specify and place each selected report on a separate worksheet in the workbook. The Solver reports are discussed in the "Creating Solver Reports" section later in this chapter.

Click the OK button to accept the settings in the Solver Results dialog box, or click the Cancel button to restore the model's cells' original values and ignore any settings in the Solver Results dialog box.

You can also click the Save Scenario button to open the Save Scenario dialog box, where you can save cell values for use with the Scenario Manager dialog box. For details on working with the Scenario Manager dialog box, see Chapter 3.

Working with the Show Trial Solution Dialog Box

If Solver reaches a model's specified maximum time limit or number of iterations before it finds a solution, or if the Solver Option's dialog box's Show Iteration Results check box is selected, Solver displays the Show Trial Solution dialog box, as shown in Figure 4-10.

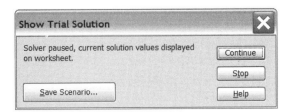

Figure 4-10. *The Show Trial Solution dialog box*

The Show Trial Solution dialog box will display one of the following messages:

Solver Paused, Current Solution Values Displayed on Worksheet: This message appears if the Solver Options dialog box's Show Iteration Results check box is selected or you press the Esc key to interrupt Solver.

The Maximum Iteration Limit Was Reached; Continue Anyway?: This message appears when Solver has completed the maximum number of iterations allowed in the Solver Options dialog box's Iterations box.

The Maximum Time Limit Was Reached; Continue Anyway?: This message appears when Solver has run for the maximum number of seconds allowed in the Solver Options dialog box's Max Time box.

In the Show Trial Solution dialog box, you can either click the Stop button to stop Solver's solution process and display the Solver Results dialog box, or click the Continue button to have Solver continue the solution process and display its next trial solution. You can also click the Save Scenario button to save the current trial solution's results as a scenario.

Creating Solver Reports

If Solver finds a solution, Solver allows you to create one or a combination of the following types of reports:

- The Answer report lists the model's target cell and the adjustable cells with their original and final values, and information about the model's constraints.

- The Sensitivity report lists how sensitive the solution is to small changes in the target cell's formula or the model's constraints. Use this type of report for problems that do not contain integer constraints.

- The Limits report lists the model's target cell and the adjustable cells with their respective values, lower and upper limits, and target values. Use this type of report for problems that do not contain integer constraints.

To create a report, click one or more report types in the Reports box in the Solver Results dialog box (see Figure 4-9, shown earlier in the chapter), and then click OK. The corresponding reports are created on new worksheets in the current workbook, one report per new worksheet.

Interpreting the Answer Report

The Answer report, shown in Figure 4-11, lists the following:

- The target cell's and adjustable cells' address, their names if ones were assigned, their original values before Solver was run, and their final values after Solver was run

- The constraints' cell addresses, their names if ones were assigned, the cells' values, the constraints' formulas, the constraints' statuses (Binding, meaning a slack value of 0, or Not Binding, meaning a nonzero slack value), and the constraints' slack values

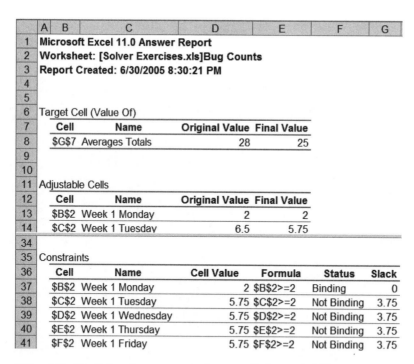

	A	B	C	D	E	F	G
1	Microsoft Excel 11.0 Answer Report						
2	Worksheet: [Solver Exercises.xls]Bug Counts						
3	Report Created: 6/30/2005 8:30:21 PM						
4							
5							
6	Target Cell (Value Of)						
7		Cell	Name	Original Value	Final Value		
8		$G$7	Averages Totals	28	25		
9							
10							
11	Adjustable Cells						
12		Cell	Name	Original Value	Final Value		
13		$B$2	Week 1 Monday	2	2		
14		$C$2	Week 1 Tuesday	6.5	5.75		
34							
35	Constraints						
36		Cell	Name	Cell Value	Formula	Status	Slack
37		$B$2	Week 1 Monday	2	$B$2>=2	Binding	0
38		$C$2	Week 1 Tuesday	5.75	$C$2>=2	Not Binding	3.75
39		$D$2	Week 1 Wednesday	5.75	$D$2>=2	Not Binding	3.75
40		$E$2	Week 1 Thursday	5.75	$E$2>=2	Not Binding	3.75
41		$F$2	Week 1 Friday	5.75	$F$2>=2	Not Binding	3.75

Figure 4-11. *The Solver Answer report (panes split for readability)*

A *slack value* is the absolute difference in values between the left side and the right side of the constraint. The left side of the constraint is the constraint cell's value, and the right side of the constraint is a specific value or the value of another specified cell. For example, for a constraint $C$2 >= 2, the slack value is the difference between the value in cell C2 and the number 2. For a constraint $A$5 >= $C$2, the slack value is the difference between the values in cells A5 and C2.

Interpreting the Sensitivity Report

The Sensitivity report (available only for problems that do not contain integer constraints), shown in Figure 4-12, lists the following:

- The adjustable cells' addresses and their names if ones were assigned

- The adjustable cells' final values after Solver was run

- The reduced cost, which is the change in the optimum problem's outcome per unit change in the upper or lower bounds of the variable

- The objective coefficient, which measures the relative relationship between the changing cell and the target cell (for example, if a changing cell's value is 1.32, and the target cell's value is 96, the objective coefficient will be 1.32 divided by 96, or 0.01375)

- The allowable increase and allowable decrease, which indicate how much the problem's objective coefficient can change before the optimum solution changes

---

▓**Note** The limit of 1E+30 appearing in a Solver report is Solver's way of indicating that any increase is allowable. Similarly, it displays 1E-30 to indicate that any decrease is allowable.

- The constraints' cell addresses and their names if ones were assigned

- The constraints' cells' final values after Solver was run

- The shadow price, which indicates how much the problem's objective outcome will change if you change the right-hand side of the corresponding constraint by one unit, within the limits given in the Allowable Increase and Allowable Decrease columns

- The right-hand side of the constraint (in the Constraint R.H. Side column), which indicates whether it is a specific value or another cell reference

- The allowable increase and allowable decrease, which indicate how much the constraint limit can change and still yield an optimal solution

	A	B	C	D	E	F	G	H
1		Microsoft Excel 11.0 Sensitivity Report						
2		Worksheet: [Solver Exercises.xls]Baking Cupcakes						
3		Report Created: 6/30/2005 8:29:26 PM						
4								
5								
6		Adjustable Cells						
7				Final	Reduced	Objective	Allowable	Allowable
8		Cell	Name	Value	Cost	Coefficient	Increase	Decrease
9		$B$12	Cupcakes	96	0	0.01375	1E+30	0.01375
10								
11		Constraints						
12				Final	Shadow	Constraint	Allowable	Allowable
13		Cell	Name	Value	Price	R.H. Side	Increase	Decrease
14		$B$5	(Cupcakes/24)*3	12	0.11	12	1E+30	1E+30

Figure 4-12. *The Solver Sensitivity report*

Interpreting the Limits Report

The Limits report (available only for problems that do not contain integer constraints) shown in Figure 4-13, lists the ranges of values over which the maximum and minimum objective values can be found. The lower limit is the smallest values that the changing cells can contain and still satisfy the constraints, and the upper limit is the largest values that the changing cells can contain and still satisfy the constraints.

	A	B	C	D	E	F	G	H	I	J
1		Microsoft Excel 11.0 Limits Report								
2		Worksheet: [Solver Exercises.xls]Limits Report 3								
3		Report Created: 6/30/2005 8:30:21 PM								
4										
5										
6			Target							
7		Cell	Name	Value						
8		$G$7	Averages Totals	25						
9										
10										
11			Adjustable			Lower	Target		Upper	Target
12		Cell	Name	Value		Limit	Result		Limit	Result
13		$B$2	Week 1 Monday	2		2	25		2	25
14		$C$2	Week 1 Tuesday	5.75		2	24.0625		10	26.0625
30		$D$5	Week 4 Wednesday	5.75		2	24.0625		10	26.0625
31		$E$5	Week 4 Thursday	5.75		2	24.0625		10	26.0625
32		$F$5	Week 4 Friday	5.75		2	24.0625		10	26.0625

Figure 4-13. *The Solver Limits report (panes split for readability)*

You can put what you've learned about Solver into practice in the previous sections through the following Try It exercises.

Try It: Use Solver to Solve Math Problems

In this set of exercises, you will use Solver to solve some simple math problems. These exercises are included in the Excel workbook named Solver Try It Exercises.xls, which is available for download from the Source Code area of the Apress web site (http://www.apress.com). The data for this set of exercises is on the workbook's Math Problems worksheet, shown in Figure 4-14.

	A	B	C
1	Math Problem 1: Volume		
2			
3	Length	3	
4	Width	4	
5	Height	5	
6	Volume	60	← B3*B4*B5
7			
8	Math Problem 2: Velocity		
9			
10	Time (minutes)	130	
11	Speed (km/h)	75	
12	Distance (km)	162.5	← (B10/60)*B11

Figure 4-14. *The Math Problems worksheet*

The Math Problems worksheet consists of two parts. The upper part of the worksheet is used to calculate a cube's length, width, height, and volume. The lower part of the worksheet is used to calculate an object's time, speed, and distance traveled.

Cube Volume Problem

First, use Solver to determine a cube's volume. Assume a width of at least 4 units; an area of exactly 80 units; and whole numbers for the length, width, and height.

1. Click Tools ➤ Solver.

2. Click Reset All, and then click OK.

3. Click the Set Target cell box, and then click or type cell **B6**.

4. Click the Value Of option. In the Value Of box, type **80**.

5. Click the By Changing Cells box, and then select cells B3 through B5.

6. Click Add.

7. Click the Cell Reference box, and then click or type cell **B4**.

8. In the operator box, select =.

9. Click the Constraint box, and then type **4**.

10. Click Add.

11. Click the Cell Reference box, and then select cells B3 through B5.

12. In the operator box, select Int.

13. Click OK. Your Solver Parameters dialog box should look like Figure 4-15.

14. Click Solve, and then click OK.

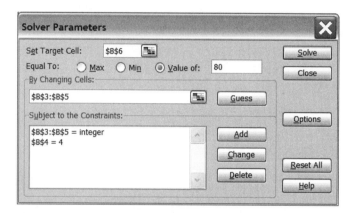

Figure 4-15. *The completed Solver Parameters dialog box for the first math problem*

Compare your results to Figure 4-16.

	A	B
1	Math Problem 1: Volume	
2		
3	Length	4
4	Width	4
5	Height	5
6	Volume	80

Figure 4-16. *The Math Problems worksheet after using Solver to determine a cube's volume, given several constraints*

Object Velocity Problem

Next, use Solver to determine how long it might take an object to travel 125 kilometers, provided that the object may not exceed 70 kilometers per hour.

1. Click Tools ➤ Solver.

2. Click Reset All, and then click OK.

3. Click the Set Target cell box, and then click or type cell **B12**.

4. Click the Value Of option. In the Value Of box, type **125**.

5. Click the By Changing Cells box, and then select cells B10 and B11.

6. Click Add.

7. Click the Cell Reference box, and then click or type cell **B11**.

8. In the operator box, select =.

9. Click the Constraint box, and then type **70**.

10. Click OK. Your Solver Parameters dialog box should look like Figure 4-17.

11. Click Solve, and then click OK.

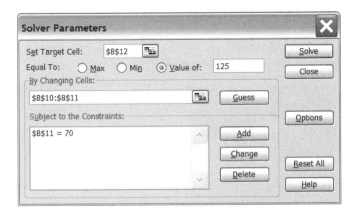

Figure 4-17. *The completed Solver Parameters dialog box for the second math problem*

Compare your results to Figure 4-18.

8	Math Problem 2: Velocity	
9		
10	Time (minutes)	107.14
11	Speed (km/h)	70
12	Distance (km)	125

Figure 4-18. *The Math Problems worksheet after using Solver to determine an object's time, speed, and distance traveled*

Try It: Use Solver to Forecast Auction Prices

In this set of exercises, you will use Solver to forecast auction prices for an online auction web site. The data for this set of exercises is on the Solver Try It Exercises.xls workbook's Online Auction worksheet, shown in Figure 4-19.

	A	B	C	D	E	F	G
1	Jewelry Item Description	Starting Bid	Bid Increment	Number of Bids	Current Bid	Days Bid Has Been Open	Bid Increase Per Day
2	Earrings	$12.00	$2.00	7	$26.00	5	$2.80
3	Pendant	$35.00	$5.00	6	$65.00	4	$7.50
4	Engagement Ring	$95.00	$7.50	12	$185.00	3	$30.00
5	Wedding Ring	$125.00	$10.00	4	$165.00	10	$4.00
6	Wedding Set	$205.00	$12.50	3	$242.50	9	$4.17
7	Averages	$94.40	$7.40	6.4	$136.70	6.2	$9.69

Figure 4-19. *The Online Auction worksheet*

The Online Auction worksheet consists of the following:

- Each jewelry item's description (column A)

- Each jewelry item's starting auction bid (column B)

- The dollar amount by which each subsequent auction bid for each jewelry item can be raised (column C)

- The number of auction bids for each jewelry item (column D)

- Each jewelry item's current bid (column E)

- The number of consecutive days that the bidding period for each jewelry item has remained open (column F)

- Each jewelry item's average daily auction bid increase (column G)

Average Daily Bid Increase for One Item

First, use Solver to forecast an average daily auction bid increase of $4.00 for earrings with an auction length of six days.

1. Click Tools ➤ Solver.

2. Click Reset All, and then click OK.

3. Click the Set Target cell box, and then click or type cell **G2**.

4. Click the Value Of option. In the Value Of box, type **4**.

5. Click the By Changing Cells box. Then click cell D2, press and hold down the Ctrl key, and click cell F2.

6. Click Add.

7. Click the Cell Reference box, and then click or type cell **F2**.

8. In the operator box, select =.

9. Click the Constraint box, and then type **6**.

10. Click OK. Your Solver Parameters dialog box should look like Figure 4-20.

11. Click Solve, and then click OK.

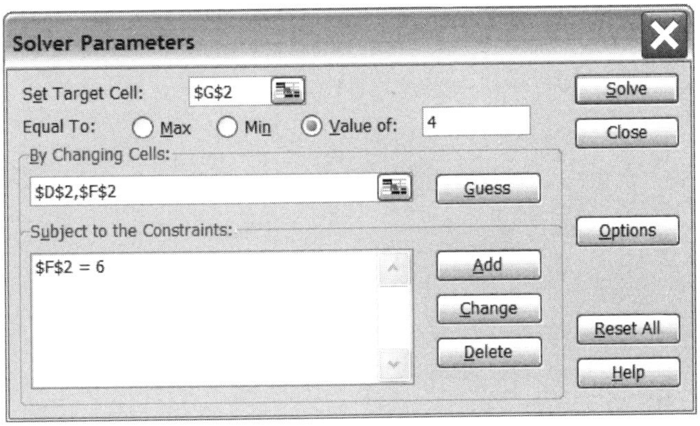

Figure 4-20. *The completed Solver Parameters dialog box for the first online auction problem*

Compare your results to Figure 4-21.

	A	B	C	D	E	F	G
1	Jewelry Item Description	Starting Bid	Bid Increment	Number of Bids	Current Bid	Days Bid Has Been Open	Bid Increase Per Day
2	Earrings	$12.00	$2.00	12	$36.00	6	$4.00
3	Pendant	$35.00	$5.00	6	$65.00	4	$7.50
4	Engagement Ring	$95.00	$7.50	12	$185.00	3	$30.00
5	Wedding Ring	$125.00	$10.00	4	$165.00	10	$4.00
6	Wedding Set	$205.00	$12.50	3	$242.50	9	$4.17
7	Averages	$94.40	$7.40	7.4	$138.70	6.4	$9.93

Figure 4-21. *The Online Auction worksheet after using Solver to determine the earrings' average daily auction bid increase, given several constraints*

Average Daily Auction Bid Increase for All Items

Next, use Solver to forecast an average daily auction bid increase of $12.00 for all current online auction items, given the following constraints:

- No individual jewelry auction item can have fewer than 3 or more than 12 total bids.

- No individual jewelry auction item can be open for fewer than 3 or more than 10 days.

- The total number of auction bids and the total number of open days for each individual jewelry auction item must be a whole number.

■**Note** This exercise assumes that you have already completed the previous exercise and are starting with the worksheet values shown in Figure 4-21.

---

1. Click Tools ➤ Solver.

2. Click Reset All, and then click OK.

3. Click the Set Target cell box, and then click or type cell **G7**.

4. Click the Value Of option. In the Value Of box, type **12**.

5. Click the By Changing Cells box. Then select cells D2 through D6, press and hold down the Ctrl key, and select cells F2 through F6.

6. Click Add.

7. Click the Cell Reference box, and then select cells D2 through D6.

8. Click the Constraint box, and then type **12**.

9. Click Add.

10. Click the Cell Reference box, and then select cells D2 through D6 again.

11. In the operator box, select >=.

12. Click the Constraint box, and then type **3**.

13. Click Add.

14. Click the Cell Reference box, and then select cells D2 through D6 again.

15. In the operator box, select Int.

16. Click Add.

17. Click the Cell Reference box, and then select cells F2 through F6.

18. Click the Constraint box, and then type **10**.

19. Click Add.

20. Click the Cell Reference box, and then select cells F2 through F6 again.

21. In the operator box, select >=.

22. Click the Constraint box, and then type **3**.

23. Click Add.

24. Click the Cell Reference box, and then select cells F2 through F6 again.

25. In the operator box, select Int.

26. Click OK. Your Solver Parameters dialog box should look like Figure 4-22.

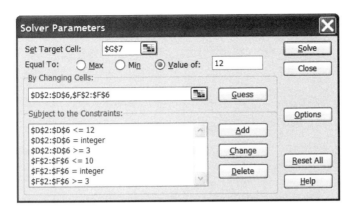

Figure 4-22. *The completed Solver Parameters dialog box for the second online auction problem*

27. Click Solve, and then click OK.

Compare your results to Figure 4-23.

	A	B	C	D	E	F	G
1	Jewelry Item Description	Starting Bid	Bid Increment	Number of Bids	Current Bid	Days Bid Has Been Open	Bid Increase Per Day
2	Earrings	$12.00	$2.00	5	$22.00	3	$3.33
3	Pendant	$35.00	$5.00	6	$65.00	3	$10.00
4	Engagement Ring	$95.00	$7.50	7	$147.50	3	$17.50
5	Wedding Ring	$125.00	$10.00	5	$175.00	3	$16.67
6	Wedding Set	$205.00	$12.50	3	$242.50	3	$12.50
7	Averages	$94.40	$7.40	5.2	$130.40	3.0	$12.00

Figure 4-23. *The Online Auction worksheet after using Solver to determine the average daily auction bid increase for all current auction items, given several constraints*

Try It: Use Solver to Determine a Home Sales Price

In this exercise, you will use Solver to determine a target home sales price. This exercise's data is on the Solver Try It Exercises.xls workbook's Home Sales worksheet, shown in Figure 4-24.

	A	B	C
1	Loan Amount	$200,000	
2	Term in Months	480	
3	Interest Rate	5.75%	
4	Monthly Payment	($1,065.78)	← PMT(B3/12, B2, B1)

Figure 4-24. *The Home Sales worksheet*

The Home Sales worksheet consists of the following:

- The total home's mortgage amount (cell B1)

- The mortgage's term in months (cell B2)

- The mortgage's interest rate (cell B3)

- The mortgage's monthly payment (cell B4)

To keep it simple, assume the mortgage amount is the same as the target home sales price, and assume the monthly payment covers all aspects of the mortgage, including all taxes and fees held in escrow.

Use Solver to determine the target home sales price given a payment of no more than $1,500.00, an interest rate of no more than 5.75%, and a 30-year (360-month) mortgage term.

1. Click Tools ➤ Solver.

2. Click Reset All, and then click OK.

3. Click the Set Target cell box, and then click or type cell **B4**.

4. Click the Max option.

5. Click the By Changing Cells box, and then select cells B1 through B3.

6. Click Add.

7. Click the Cell Reference box, and then click or type cell **B2**.

8. In the operator box, select =.

9. Click the Constraint box, and then type **360**.

10. Click Add.

11. Click the Cell Reference box, and then click or type cell **B3**.

12. In the operator box, select =.

13. Click the Constraint box, and then type **0.0575**.

14. Click Add.

15. Click the Cell Reference box, and then click or type cell **B4**.

16. Click the Constraint box, and then type **-1500**.

17. Click OK. Your Solver Parameters dialog box should look like Figure 4-25.

18. Click Solve, and then click OK.

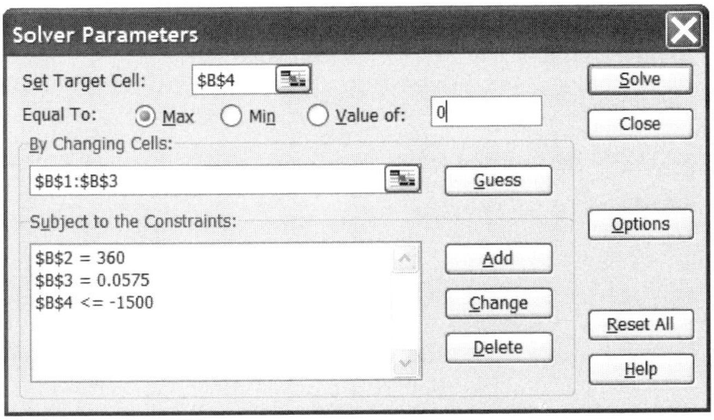

Figure 4-25. *The completed Solver Parameters dialog box for the target home sales price problem*

Compare your results to Figure 4-26.

	A	B
1	Loan Amount	$257,037
2	Term in Months	360
3	Interest Rate	5.75%
4	Monthly Payment	($1,500.00)

Figure 4-26. *The Home Sales worksheet after using Solver to determine the target home sales price, given several constraints*

Try It: Use Solver to Forecast the Weather

In this set of exercises, you will use Solver to forecast the weather. The data for these exercises is on the Solver Try It Exercises.xls workbook's Weather worksheet, shown in Figure 4-27.

	A	B	C	D	E	F	K	L	M	N	O	P
1	City	State	Jan	Feb	Mar	Apr	Sep	Oct	Nov	Dec	Total	Average
2	Bakersfield	CA	0.9	1.1	1.0	0.6	0.2	0.3	0.7	0.6	5.7	0.5
3	Bishop	CA	1.1	1.0	0.4	0.3	0.2	0.1	0.6	0.8	5.4	0.4
4	Eureka	CA	6.0	4.7	5.3	2.9	0.9	2.7	6.4	6.0	37.5	3.1
5	Fresno	CA	2.0	1.8	1.9	1.0	0.2	0.5	1.4	1.4	10.6	0.9
6	Long Beach	CA	2.5	2.5	2.0	0.7	0.3	0.3	1.7	1.7	11.8	1.0
22	Salem	OR	5.9	4.5	4.2	2.4	1.6	3.0	6.3	6.8	39.2	3.3
23	Olympia	WA	8.0	5.8	5.0	3.3	2.3	4.3	8.1	8.1	50.6	4.2
24	Seattle	WA	5.4	4.0	3.5	2.3	1.9	3.2	5.8	5.9	37.2	3.1
25	Spokane	WA	2.0	1.5	1.5	1.2	0.7	1.0	2.2	2.4	16.5	1.4
26	Yakima	WA	1.2	0.7	0.7	0.5	0.4	0.5	1.0	1.4	8.0	0.7
27	Averages		3.9	3.1	2.9	1.6	0.8	1.6	3.6	3.7	23.6	2.0

Figure 4-27. *The Weather worksheet (panes split for readability)*

The Weather worksheet consists of the following:

- The city and state names in which precipitation totals were collected (columns A and B)

- The monthly precipitation totals for each city (columns C through N)

- The yearly precipitation totals for each city (column O)

- The average monthly precipitation for each city (column P)

- The average monthly precipitation for each month (row 27)

Minimum Yearly Precipitation Total for Seattle

First, use Solver to forecast the minimum yearly precipitation total for Seattle. Assume a yearly precipitation total target of 40 inches; no monthly precipitation total of less than 2 inches; and no less than 5 inches in January, February, November, or December.

1. Click Tools ➤ Solver.

2. Click Reset All, and then click OK.

3. Click the Set Target cell box, and then click or type cell **O24**.

4. Click the Value Of option. In the Value Of box, type **40**.

5. Click the By Changing Cells box, and then select cells C24 through N24.

6. Click Add.

7. Click the Cell Reference box, and then select cells C24 through N24.

8. In the operator box, select >=.

9. Click the Constraint box, and then type **2**.

10. Click Add.

11. Click the Cell Reference box, and then select cells C24 and D24.

12. In the operator box, select >=.

13. Click the Constraint box, and then type **5**.

14. Click Add.

15. Click the Cell Reference box, and then select cells M24 and N24.

16. In the operator box, select >=.

17. Click the Constraint box, and then type **5**.

18. Click OK. Your Solver Parameters dialog box should look like Figure 4-28.

19. Click Solve, and then click OK.

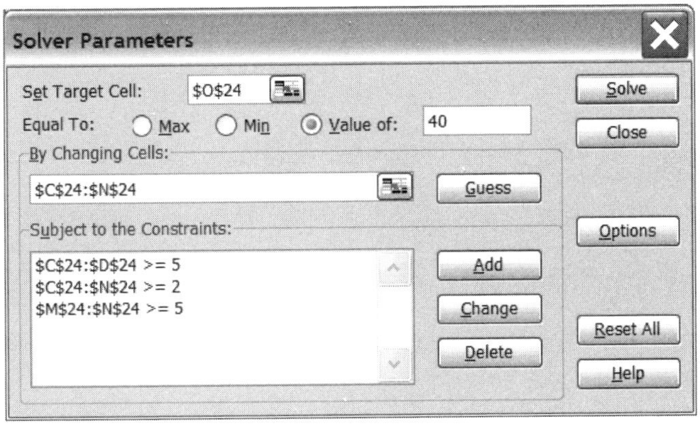

Figure 4-28. *The completed Solver Parameters dialog box for the first weather problem*

Compare your results to Figure 4-29.

	A	B	C	D	E	F		K	L	M	N	O	P
1	City	State	Jan	Feb	Mar	Apr		Sep	Oct	Nov	Dec	Total	Average
24	Seattle	**WA**	**5.2**	**5.0**	**3.3**	**2.1**		**2.0**	**3.0**	**5.6**	**5.7**	**40.0**	**3.3**
25	Spokane	WA	2.0	1.5	1.5	1.2		0.7	1.0	2.2	2.4	16.5	1.4
26	Yakima	WA	1.2	0.7	0.7	0.5		0.4	0.5	1.0	1.4	8.0	0.7
27	Averages		3.8	3.1	2.9	1.6		0.9	1.6	3.6	3.7	23.7	2.0

Figure 4-29. *The Weather worksheet after using Solver to forecast the weather for Seattle, given several constraints (panes split for readability)*

Average December Precipitation Total for All Cities

Next, use Solver to forecast the average December yearly precipitation total for all cities. Assume a yearly precipitation combined average of 3 inches, with no monthly precipitation totals of less than 1 inch or more than 10 inches.

■**Note** This exercise assumes that you have already completed the previous exercise and are starting with the worksheet values shown in Figure 4-29.

1. Click Tools ➤ Solver.

2. Click Reset All, and then click OK.

3. Click the Set Target cell box, and then click or type cell **N27**.

4. Click the Value Of option. In the Value Of box, type **3**.

5. Click the By Changing Cells box, and then select cells N2 through N26.

6. Click Add.

7. Click the Cell Reference box, and then select cells N2 through N26 again.

8. Click the Constraint box, and then type **10**.

9. Click Add.

10. Click the Cell Reference box, and then select cells N2 through N26 again.

11. In the operator box, select >=.

12. Click the Constraint box, and then type **1**.

13. Click OK. Your Solver Parameters dialog box should look like Figure 4-30.

14. Click Solve, and then click OK.

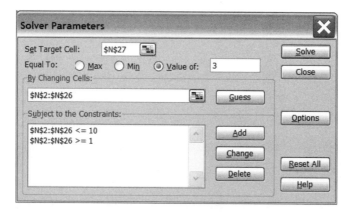

Figure 4-30. *The completed Solver Parameters dialog box for the second weather problem*

Compare your results to Figure 4-31.

	A	B	C	D	E	F	K	L	M	N	O	P
1	City	State	Jan	Feb	Mar	Apr	Sep	Oct	Nov	**Dec**	Total	Average
2	Bakersfield	CA	0.9	1.1	1.0	0.6	0.2	0.3	0.7	**1.0**	6.1	0.5
3	Bishop	CA	1.1	1.0	0.4	0.3	0.2	0.1	0.6	**1.0**	5.5	0.5
4	Eureka	CA	6.0	4.7	5.3	2.9	0.9	2.7	6.4	**5.2**	36.6	3.1
5	Fresno	CA	2.0	1.8	1.9	1.0	0.2	0.5	1.4	**1.0**	10.2	0.8
6	Long Beach	CA	2.5	2.5	2.0	0.7	0.3	0.3	1.7	**1.0**	11.1	0.9
22	Salem	OR	5.9	4.5	4.2	2.4	1.6	3.0	6.3	**5.9**	38.3	3.2
23	Olympia	WA	8.0	5.8	5.0	3.3	2.3	4.3	8.1	**7.2**	49.7	4.1
24	Seattle	WA	5.2	5.0	3.3	2.1	2.0	3.0	5.6	**4.8**	39.1	3.3
25	Spokane	WA	2.0	1.5	1.5	1.2	0.7	1.0	2.2	**1.5**	15.6	1.3
26	Yakima	WA	1.2	0.7	0.7	0.5	0.4	0.5	1.0	**1.0**	7.6	0.6
27	Averages		3.8	3.1	2.9	1.6	0.9	1.6	3.6	**3.0**	23.0	1.9

Figure 4-31. *The Weather worksheet after using Solver to forecast the December weather for all cities, given several constraints (panes split for readability)*

Following is a series of seven more involved Solver samples for you to try.

Try It: Experiment with the Default Solver Samples

Excel includes a series of Solver samples that you can experiment with to learn more about how to use Solver. These samples can be found in the SOLVSAMP.XLS file. This file is usually located in the <*drive*>:\Program Files\Microsoft Office\OFFICE11\SAMPLES folder or the <*drive*>:\Program Files\Microsoft Office\Office\SAMPLES folder. This file is installed with Microsoft Office Excel 2003 when you perform a Complete installation (or a Custom installation and select Advanced Customization ➤ Microsoft Office ➤ Microsoft Office Excel ➤ Sample Files).

■**Note** For earlier Office versions, you can usually find the SOLVSAMP.XLS file in the <*drive*>:\Program Files\ Microsoft Office\Office\SAMPLES folder or the <*drive*>:\Office\Examples\Solver folder.

The following sections describe the SOLVSAMP.XLS file's seven worksheets and provide exercises for you to experiment with these Solver samples. After you complete each example, in the Solver Results dialog box, click Restore Original Values, and then click OK to discard the results and return the cells to their former values. This way, the sample worksheets will not be changed by your experiments.

Quick Tour

The first worksheet, labeled Quick Tour and partially shown in Figure 4-32, is a marketing model that shows sales rising from a base figure along with increases in advertising, but with diminishing returns. For instance, the first $10,000 of advertising in quarter 1 (Q1), in cell B11, yields about 3,600 incremental units sold (cell B5), but the next $10,000 yields only about 800 units more (cell C5).

	A	B	C	D	E	F
1	**Quick Tour of Microsoft Excel Solver**					
2	Month	Q1	Q2	Q3	Q4	Total
3	Seasonality	0.9	1.1	0.8	1.2	
4						
5	Units Sold	3,592	4,390	3,192	4,789	15,962
6	Sales Revenue	$143,662	$175,587	$127,700	$191,549	$638,498
7	Cost of Sales	89,789	109,742	79,812	119,718	399,061
8	Gross Margin	53,873	65,845	47,887	71,831	239,437
9						
10	Salesforce	8,000	8,000	9,000	9,000	34,000
11	Advertising	10,000	10,000	10,000	10,000	40,000
12	Corp Overhead	21,549	26,338	19,155	28,732	95,775
13	Total Costs	39,549	44,338	38,155	47,732	169,775
14						
15	Prod. Profit	$14,324	$21,507	$9,732	$24,099	$69,662
16	Profit Margin	10%	12%	8%	13%	11%
17						
18	Product Price	$40.00				
19	Product Cost	$25.00				

Figure 4-32. *The Quick Tour Solver sample worksheet with its default values*

As highlighted on the worksheet by a thick cell border, one possible target cell, cell B15, represents the product profit. The product profit is simply the difference of the gross margin (cell B8) minus the total costs (cell B13).

For example, in the Quick Tour sample worksheet, you may want to know how much you could spend on advertising to generate the maximum profit for the year but with a total advertising budget of only $50,000. To figure this out using Solver, do the following:

1. Click Tools ➤ Solver.

2. Click Reset All, and then click OK.

3. Click the Set Target Cell box, and then click cell F15 (Total Product Profit).

4. Click Max.

5. Click the By Changing Cells box, and then select cells B11 through E11 (Advertising).

6. Click Add.

7. Click the Cell Reference box, and then click cell F11 (Total Advertising).

8. Click the Constraint box, and then type **50000**.

9. Click OK.

10. Click Solve.

Compare your results to Figure 4-33.

	A	B	C	D	E	F
1	**Quick Tour of Microsoft Excel Solver**					
2	Month	Q1	Q2	Q3	Q4	Total
3	Seasonality	0.9	1.1	0.8	1.2	
4						
5	Units Sold	3,486	5,208	2,755	6,198	17,646
6	Sales Revenue	$139,449	$208,313	$110,182	$247,910	$705,856
7	Cost of Sales	87,156	130,196	68,864	154,944	441,160
8	Gross Margin	52,294	78,118	41,318	92,966	264,696
9						
10	Salesforce	8,000	8,000	9,000	9,000	34,000
11	Advertising	9,249	15,298	6,678	18,776	50,000
12	Corp Overhead	20,917	31,247	16,527	37,187	105,878
13	Total Costs	38,166	54,545	32,205	64,962	189,878
14						
15	Prod. Profit	$14,127	$23,573	$9,113	$28,004	$74,817
16	Profit Margin	10%	11%	8%	11%	11%
17						
18	Product Price	$40.00				
19	Product Cost	$25.00				

Figure 4-33. *The Quick Tour Solver sample worksheet after using Solver to forecast maximized profits given an advertising budget limit of $50,000*

Product Mix

The second worksheet, labeled Product Mix and partially shown in Figure 4-34, portrays a model of parts for electronic equipment. These parts are in limited supply. You can use Solver to determine the most profitable mix of electronic equipment to build. However, the profit per electronic equipment item decreases as more items are built. This is because as each item is built, you must give equipment sellers volume discounts so that they are inclined to purchase more items from you at lower and lower prices.

	A	B	C	D	E	F	G	H
1	**Example 1: Product mix problem with diminishing profit margin.**							
2	Your company manufactures TVs, stereos and speakers, using a common parts inventory							
3	of power supplies, speaker cones, etc. Parts are in limited supply and you must determine							
4	the most profitable mix of products to build. But your profit per unit built decreases with							
5	volume because extra price incentives are needed to load the distribution channel.							
6								
7								
8				*TV set*	*Stereo*	*Speaker*		
9			*Number to Build->*	100	100	100		
10	*Part Name*	*Inventory*	*No. Used*					
11	*Chassis*	450	200	1	1	0		
12	*Picture Tube*	250	100	1	0	0		*Diminishing*
13	*Speaker Cone*	800	500	2	2	1		*Returns*
14	*Power Supply*	450	200	1	1	0		*Exponent*
15	*Electronics*	600	400	2	1	1		0.9
16				*Profits:*				
17			*By Product*	$4,732	$3,155	$2,208		
18			Total	$10,095				

Figure 4-34. *The Product Mix Solver sample worksheet with its default values*

To use Solver to determine the most profitable mix of electronic equipment to build, do the following:

1. Click Tools ➤ Solver.

2. Click Reset All, and then click OK to clear Solver's existing settings.

3. Click the Set Target Cell box, and then click cell D18 (Total Profits By Product).

4. Click Max.

5. Click the By Changing Cells box, and then select cells D9 through F9 (Number to Build for TV Sets, Stereos, and Speakers).

6. Click Add.

7. Click the Cell Reference box, and then select cells C11 through C15 (Number Used).

8. Click the Constraint box, and then select cells B11 through B15 (Inventory).

9. Click Add. This constraint ensures that you will not allocate more parts than are in your inventory.

10. Click the Cell Reference box, and then select cells D9 through F9 (Number to Build for TV Sets, Stereos, and Speakers).

11. In the operator list, select >=.

12. Click the Constraint box, and then type the number **0**.

13. Click OK. This constraint ensures that you will not produce a negative number of electronic items in any category.

14. Click Options.

15. Clear the Assume Linear Model check box, and then click OK. You need to do this because the model is nonlinear (due to the factor in cell H15, which shows that profit per unit diminishes with volume).

16. Click Solve.

Compare your results to Figure 4-35.

	A	B	C	D	E	F	G	H
1	**Example 1: Product mix problem with diminishing profit margin.**							
2	Your company manufactures TVs, stereos and speakers, using a common parts inventory							
3	of power supplies, speaker cones, etc. Parts are in limited supply and you must determine							
4	the most profitable mix of products to build. But your profit per unit built decreases with							
5	volume because extra price incentives are needed to load the distribution channel.							
6								
7								
8				*TV set*	*Stereo*	*Speaker*		
9			Number to Build->	160	200	80		
10	*Part Name*	*Inventory*	*No. Used*					
11	*Chassis*	450	360	1	1	0		
12	*Picture Tube*	250	160	1	0	0		*Diminishing*
13	*Speaker Cone*	800	800	2	2	1		*Returns*
14	*Power Supply*	450	360	1	1	0		*Exponent*
15	*Electronics*	600	600	2	1	1		0.9
16			*Profits:*					
17			*By Product*	$7,220	$5,887	$1,811		
18			Total	$14,917				

Figure 4-35. *The Product Mix Solver sample worksheet after using Solver to forecast the most profitable mix of electronic equipment to build given several constraints*

Shipping Routes

The third worksheet, labeled Shipping Routes and partially shown in Figure 4-36, is a model that describes shipping goods from production plants to warehouses. You can use Solver to minimize the associated shipping costs, while also not exceeding the supply available from each plant to meet the demand from each warehouse.

	A	B	C	D	E	F	G	H
1	**Example 2: Transportation Problem.**							
2	Minimize the costs of shipping goods from production plants to warehouses near metropolitan demand							
3	centers, while not exceeding the supply available from each plant and meeting the demand from each							
4	metropolitan area.							
6			*Number to ship from plant x to warehouse y (at intersection):*					
7	*Plants:*	*Total*	*San Fran*	*Denver*	*Chicago*	*Dallas*	*New York*	
8	S. Carolina	5	1	1	1	1	1	
9	Tennessee	5	1	1	1	1	1	
10	Arizona	5	1	1	1	1	1	
11			—	—	—	—	—	
12	Totals:		3	3	3	3	3	
14	*Demands by Whse →*		180	80	200	160	220	
15	*Plants:*	*Supply*	*Shipping costs from plant x to warehouse y (at intersection):*					
16	S. Carolina	310	10	8	6	5	4	
17	Tennessee	260	6	5	4	3	6	
18	Arizona	280	3	4	5	5	9	
20	*Shipping:*	**$83**	$19	$17	$15	$13	$19	

Figure 4-36. *The Shipping Routes Solver sample worksheet with its default values*

To use Solver to minimize the associated shipping costs while meeting warehouse demands, do the following:

1. Click Tools ➤ Solver.

2. Click Reset All, and then click OK to clear Solver's existing settings.

3. Click the Set Target Cell box, and then click cell B20 (Total Shipping).

4. Click Min.

5. Click the By Changing Cells box, and then select cells C8 through G10 (Number to Ship from Plants to Warehouses).

6. Click Add.

7. Click the Cell Reference box, and then select cells B8 through B10 (Total Shipped from Plants).

8. Click the Constraint box, and then select cells B16 through B18 (Total Supply).

9. Click Add. This constraint ensures that you will not ship more units than you have in your inventory.

10. Click the Cell Reference box, and then select cells C12 through G12 (Total Shipped to Warehouses).

11. In the operator list, click >=.

12. Click the Constraint box, and then select cells C14 through G14 (Total Demands by Warehouse).

13. Click Add. This constraint ensures that you will not ship more units to warehouses than you have demands by your warehouses.

14. Click the Cell Reference box, and then select cells C8 through G10 (Number to Ship from Plants to Warehouses).

15. In the operator list, click >=.

16. Click the Constraint box, and then type the number **0**.

17. Click OK. This constraint ensures that you will not ship negative units to warehouses.

18. Click Options.

19. Select the Assume Linear Model check box, and then click OK. You can select this option because the model is linear.

20. Click Solve.

Compare your results to Figure 4-37.

	A	B	C	D	E	F	G	H
1	**Example 2: Transportation Problem.**							
2	Minimize the costs of shipping goods from production plants to warehouses near metropolitan demand							
3	centers, while not exceeding the supply available from each plant and meeting the demand from each							
4	metropolitan area.							
6			*Number to ship from plant x to warehouse y (at intersection):*					
7	*Plants:*	*Total*	*San Fran*	*Denver*	*Chicago*	*Dallas*	*New York*	
8	S. Carolina	300	0	0	0	80	220	
9	Tennessee	260	0	0	180	80	0	
10	Arizona	280	180	80	20	0	0	
11			—	—	—	—	—	
12	Totals:		180	80	200	160	220	
13								
14	*Demands by Whse →*		180	80	200	160	220	
15	*Plants:*	*Supply:*	*Shipping costs from plant x to warehouse y (at intersection):*					
16	S. Carolina	310	10	8	6	5	4	
17	Tennessee	260	6	5	4	3	6	
18	Arizona	280	3	4	5	5	9	
19								
20	*Shipping:*	**$3,200**	$540	$320	$820	$640	$880	

Figure 4-37. *The Shipping Routes Solver sample worksheet after using Solver to forecast minimized shipping costs while meeting warehouse demands, given several constraints*

Staff Scheduling

The fourth worksheet, labeled Staff Scheduling and partially shown in Figure 4-38, is a model that describes personnel scheduling for an amusement park. The goal for this model is to schedule employees working five consecutive days with two days off in such a way to meet demand from attendance levels while minimizing payroll costs. In this example, all employees are paid at the same rate, so by minimizing the number of employees working each day, you also minimize costs. Each employee works five consecutive days, followed by two days off.

	A	B	C	D	E	F	G	H	I	J	K	L
1	**Example 3: Personnel scheduling for an Amusement Park.**											
2	For employees working five consecutive days with two days off, find the schedule that meets demand											
3	from attendance levels while minimizing payroll costs.											
6	*Sch.*	*Days off*		*Employees*		*Sun*	*Mon*	*Tue*	*Wed*	*Thu*	*Fri*	*Sat*
7	*A*	*Sunday, Monday*		4		0	0	1	1	1	1	1
8	*B*	*Monday, Tuesday*		4		1	0	0	1	1	1	1
9	*C*	*Tuesday, Wed.*		4		1	1	0	0	1	1	1
10	*D*	*Wed., Thursday*		6		1	1	1	0	0	1	1
11	*E*	*Thursday, Friday*		6		1	1	1	1	0	0	1
12	*F*	*Friday, Saturday*		4		1	1	1	1	1	0	1
13	*G*	*Saturday, Sunday*		4		0	1	1	1	1	1	0
15		*Schedule Totals:*		32		24	24	24	22	20	22	28
17		*Total Demand:*				22	17	13	14	15	18	24
19		Pay/Employee/Day:		$40								
20		Payroll/Week:		$1,280								

Figure 4-38. *The Staff Scheduling Solver sample worksheet with its default values*

To use Solver to schedule employees to meet demand from attendance levels while minimizing payroll costs, do the following:

1. Click Tools ➤ Solver.

2. Click Reset All, and then click OK to clear Solver's existing settings.

3. Click the Set Target Cell box, and then click cell D20 (Payroll Per Week).

4. Click Min.

5. Click the By Changing Cells box, and then select cells D7 through D13 (Total Number of Employees).

6. Click Add.

7. Click the Cell Reference box, and then select cells D7 through D13 (Total Number of Employees).

8. In the operator list, select Int.

9. Click Add. This constraint ensures that you will allocate only whole numbers for employees.

10. Click the Cell Reference box, and then select cells D7 through D13 (Total Number of Employees).

11. In the operator box, select >=.

12. Click the Constraint box, and then type the number **1**.

13. Click Add. This constraint ensures that you will schedule at least one employee per day.

14. Click the Cell Reference box, and then select cells F15 through L15 (Schedule Totals).

15. In the operator box, select >=.

16. Click the Constraint box, and then select cells F17 through L17 (Total Demand).

17. Click OK. This constraint ensures that you will have enough employees scheduled each day to cover the schedule demands.

18. Click Options.

19. Check the Assume Linear Model check box, and then click OK. You can select this option because the model is linear.

20. Click Solve.

Compare your results to Figure 4-39.

	A	B	C	D	E	F	G	H	I	J	K	L
1	**Example 3: Personnel scheduling for an Amusement Park.**											
2	For employees working five consecutive days with two days off, find the schedule that meets demand											
3	from attendance levels while minimizing payroll costs.											
6	*Sch.*	*Days off*		*Employees*		*Sun*	*Mon*	*Tue*	*Wed*	*Thu*	*Fri*	*Sat*
7	*A*	Sunday; Monday		0		0	0	1	1	1	1	1
8	*B*	Monday; Tuesday		8		1	0	0	1	1	1	1
9	*C*	Tuesday; Wed.		0		1	1	0	0	1	1	1
10	*D*	Wed., Thursday		10		1	1	1	0	0	1	1
11	*E*	Thursday; Friday		0		1	1	1	1	0	0	1
12	*F*	Friday; Saturday		7		1	1	1	1	1	0	1
13	*G*	Saturday; Sunday		0		0	1	1	1	1	1	0
15		*Schedule Totals:*		25		25	17	17	15	15	18	25
17		*Total Demand:*				22	17	13	14	15	18	24
19		Pay/Employee/Day:		$40								
20		Payroll/Week:		**$1,000**								

Figure 4-39. *The Staff Scheduling Solver sample worksheet after using Solver to forecast schedule demands from attendance levels while minimizing payroll costs, given several constraints*

Maximizing Income

The fifth worksheet, labeled Maximizing Income and partially shown in Figure 4-40, is a model that describes how to invest excess cash in one-month, three-month, and six-month certificate of deposits (CDs). You can use Solver to forecast maximized interest income while meeting company cash requirements, plus a safety margin.

	A	B	C	D	E	F	G	H
1	**Example 4: Working Capital Management.**							
2	Determine how to invest excess cash in 1-month, 3-month and 6-month CDs so as to							
3	maximize interest income while meeting company cash requirements (plus safety margin).							
4								
5		*Yield*	*Term*		*Purchase CDs in months:*			
6	*1-mo CDs:*	1.0%	1		1, 2, 3, 4, 5 and 6			*Interest*
7	*3-mo CDs:*	4.0%	3		1 and 4			*Earned:*
8	*6-mo CDs:*	9.0%	6				*Total*	**$7,700**
9								
10	*Month:*	*Month 1*	*Month 2*	*Month 3*	*Month 4*	*Month 5*	*Month 6*	*End*
11	*Init Cash:*	$400,000	$205,000	$216,000	$237,000	$158,400	$109,400	$125,400
12	*Matur CDs:*		100,000	100,000	110,000	100,000	100,000	120,000
13	*Interest:*		1,000	1,000	1,400	1,000	1,000	2,300
14	*1-mo CDs:*	100,000	100,000	100,000	100,000	100,000	100,000	
15	*3-mo CDs:*	10,000			10,000			
16	*6-mo CDs:*	10,000						
17	*Cash Uses:*	75,000	(10,000)	(20,000)	80,000	50,000	(15,000)	60,000
18	*End Cash:*	$205,000	$216,000	$237,000	$158,400	$109,400	$125,400	$187,700
19								
20			-290000					

Figure 4-40. *The Maximizing Income Solver sample worksheet with its default values*

In this example, you must trade off the higher interest rates available from longer-term investments against the flexibility provided by keeping funds in short-term investments. This model calculates ending cash based on initial cash from the previous month, inflows from maturing CDs, outflows for new CDs, and cash needed for company operations for each month. In this model, you have a total of nine decisions to make:

- The amounts to invest in one-month CDs in months 1 through 6

- The amounts to invest in three-month CDs in months 1 and 4

- The amount to invest in six-month CDs in month 1

To use Solver to forecast maximized interest income while meeting company cash requirements, do the following:

1. Click Tools ➤ Solver.

2. Click Reset All, and then click OK to clear Solver's existing settings.

3. Click the Set Target Cell box, and then click cell H8 (Total Interest Earned).

4. Click Max.

5. Click the By Changing Cells box. Then select cells B14 through G14, press and hold down the Ctrl key, and click cells B15, E15, and B16 (CD Investments for One-Month CDs in Months 1 Through 6, Three-Month CDs in Months 1 and 4, and Six-Month CDs in Month 1).

6. Click Add.

7. Click the Cell Reference box, and then select cells B14 through G14 (CD Investments for One-Month CDs in Months 1 Through 6).

8. In the operator list, select >=.

9. Click the Constraint box, and then type the number **0**.

10. Click Add. This constraint ensures that you will invest a nonzero amount for these CDs.

11. Click the Cell Reference box, and then select cells B15 and B16 (CD Investments for Three-Month CDs and Six-Month CDs in Month 1).

12. In the operator list, select >=.

13. Click the Constraint box, and then type the number **1**.

14. Click Add. This constraint ensures that you will invest a nonzero amount for these CDs.

15. Click the Cell Reference box, and then select cells B18 through H18 (Total End Cash).

16. In the operator list, select >=.

17. Click the Constraint box, and then type **100000**.

18. Click Add. This constraint ensures that you will forecast at least $100,000 in ending cash.

19. Click the Cell Reference box, and then select cell E15 (CD Investment for Three-Month CD in Month 4).

20. In the operator list, select >=.

21. Click the Constraint box, and then type the number **1**.

22. Click OK. This constraint ensures that you will invest a nonzero amount for this CD.

23. Click Options.

24. Check the Assume Linear Model check box, and then click OK.

25. Click Solve.

Compare your results to Figure 4-41.

	A	B	C	D	E	F	G	H
1	**Example 4: Working Capital Management.**							
2	Determine how to invest excess cash in 1-month, 3-month and 6-month CDs so as to							
3	maximize interest income while meeting company cash requirements (plus safety margin).							
4								
5		*Yield*	*Term*		*Purchase CDs in months:*			
6	*1-mo CDs:*	1.0%	1		1, 2, 3, 4, 5 and 6		*Interest*	
7	*3-mo CDs:*	4.0%	3		1 and 4		*Earned:*	
8	*6-mo CDs:*	9.0%	6				*Total*	**$16,531**
9								
10	*Month:*	*Month 1*	*Month 2*	*Month 3*	*Month 4*	*Month 5*	*Month 6*	*End*
11	*Init Cash:*	$400,000	$100,000	$100,000	$100,000	$100,000	$100,000	$100,000
12	*Matur CDs:*		0	10,000	125,392	49,505	0	144,708
13	*Interest:*		0	100	4,113	495	0	11,824
14	*1-mo CDs:*	0	10,000	30,100	49,505	0	15,000	
15	*3-mo CDs:*	95,292			0			
16	*6-mo CDs:*	129,708						
17	*Cash Uses:*	75,000	(10,000)	(20,000)	80,000	50,000	(15,000)	60,000
18	*End Cash:*	$100,000	$100,000	$100,000	$100,000	$100,000	$100,000	$196,531
19								
20		164123.2197						

Figure 4-41. *The Maximizing Income Solver sample worksheet after using Solver to forecast maximized interest income while meeting company cash requirements, given several constraints*

Portfolio of Securities

The sixth worksheet, labeled Portfolio of Securities and partially shown in Figure 4-42, is a model that describes an efficient securities portfolio. You can use Solver to find the allocation of funds to stocks that minimizes the portfolio risk for a given rate of return, or that maximizes the rate of return for a given level of risk.

	A	B	C	D	E	F	G	H
1	**Example 5: Efficient stock portfolio.**							
2	Find the weightings of stocks in an efficient portfolio that maximizes the portfolio rate of							
3	return for a given level of risk. This worksheet uses the Sharpe single-index model; you							
4	can also use the Markowitz method if you have covariance terms available.							
5								
6	*Risk-free rate*		6.0%		*Market variance*		3.0%	
7	*Market rate*		15.0%		*Maximum weight*		100.0%	
8								
9		*Beta*	*ResVar*		*Weight*	**Beta*	**Var.*	
10	*Stock A*	0.80	0.04		20.0%	0.160	0.002	
11	*Stock B*	1.00	0.20		20.0%	0.200	0.008	
12	*Stock C*	1.80	0.12		20.0%	0.360	0.005	
13	*Stock D*	2.20	0.40		20.0%	0.440	0.016	
14	*T-bills*	0.00	0.00		20.0%	0.000	0.000	
15								
16	*Total*				100.0%	1.160	0.030	
17					**Return**		*Variance*	
18				Portfolio Totals:	**16.4%**		**7.1%**	

Figure 4-42. *The Portfolio of Securities Solver sample worksheet with its default values*

To use Solver to maximize the rate of return, do the following:

1. Click Tools ➤ Solver.

2. Click Reset All, and then click OK to clear Solver's existing settings.

3. Click the Set Target Cell box, and then click cell E18 (Total Rate of Return).

4. Click Max.

5. Click the By Changing Cells box, and then select cells E10 through E14 (Weight of Each Stock).

6. Click Add.

7. Click the Cell Reference box, and then select cells E10 through E14 (Weight of Each Stock).

8. In the operator list, select >=.

9. Click the Constraint box, and type the number 0.

10. Click Add. This constraint ensures that you will invest a nonzero weight for at least one stock.

11. Click the Cell Reference box, and then select cell E16 (Total Stock Weight).

12. In the operator list, select =.

13. Click the Constraint box, and then type the number **1**.

14. Click Add. This constraint ensures that you will allocate total stock weights so that they all add up to 100%.

15. Click the Cell Reference box, and then select cells G18 (Total Variance).

16. Click the Constraint box, and then type **0.071**.

17. Click OK. This constraint ensures that you will have a total variance of equal to or less than 7.1%.

18. Click Options.

19. Clear the Assume Linear Model check box, and then click OK. You need to do this because the model is nonlinear.

20. Click Solve.

Compare your results to Figure 4-43.

	A	B	C	D	E	F	G	H
1	**Example 5: Efficient stock portfolio.**							
2	Find the weightings of stocks in an efficient portfolio that maximizes the portfolio rate of							
3	return for a given level of risk. This worksheet uses the Sharpe single-index model; you							
4	can also use the Markowitz method if you have covariance terms available.							
6	Risk-free rate		6.0%		Market variance		3.0%	
7	Market rate		15.0%		Maximum weight		100.0%	
9		Beta	ResVar		Weight	*Beta	*Var	
10	Stock A	0.80	0.04		41.1%	0.329	0.007	
11	Stock B	1.00	0.20		10.3%	0.103	0.002	
12	Stock C	1.80	0.12		30.8%	0.554	0.011	
13	Stock D	2.20	0.40		11.3%	0.248	0.005	
14	T-bills	0.00	0.00		6.6%	0.000	0.000	
16	Total				100.0%	1.234	0.025	
17					Return		Variance	
18				Portfolio Totals:	17.1%		7.1%	

Figure 4-43. *The Portfolio of Securities Solver sample worksheet after using Solver to maximize the rate of return, given several constraints*

Engineering Design

The seventh worksheet, labeled Engineering Design and partially shown in Figure 4-44, is a model that describes how to find the value of a resistor in an electrical circuit that will dissipate the charge to 1% of its original value within 1/20 second after the switch is closed. This model depicts an electrical circuit containing a battery, switch, capacitor, resistor, and an inductor. With the switch in the left position, the battery charges the capacitor. When the switch is in the right position, the capacitor discharges through the inductor and the resistor, both of which dissipate electrical energy. You can use Solver to pick an appropriate value for the resistor, given values for the inductor and the capacitor.

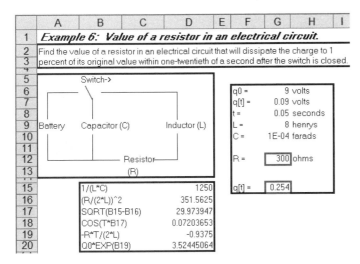

Figure 4-44. *The Engineering Design Solver sample worksheet with its default values*

To use Solver to pick the appropriate value for the resistor, do the following:

1. Click Tools ➤ Solver.

2. Click Reset All, and then click OK to clear Solver's existing settings.

3. Click the Set Target Cell box, and then click cell G15 (Total Charge at Given Time).

4. Click Value Of. Then type **0.09** in the Value Of box.

5. Click the By Changing Cells box, and then select cell G12 (Resistor).

6. Click Options.

7. Clear the Assume Linear Model check box, and click OK. (This model is nonlinear.)

8. Click Solve.

Compare your results to Figure 4-45.

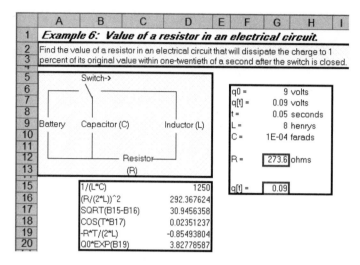

Figure 4-45. *The Engineering Design Solver sample worksheet after using Solver to forecast the appropriate value for the resistor*

Troubleshooting Solver

The following are the main scenarios in which Solver won't run, stops before it finds a solution, or reaches a solution that doesn't seem correct to you:

- You cannot run Solver because of a problem when you choose Tools ➤ Solver.

- You cannot have Solver begin finding a solution because there is a problem with a specific Solver dialog box setting.

- Once you start Solver, it cannot find a solution because it has reached some predefined limit in the model, or there is simply no possible solution to the problem.

- Solver finds a solution that you discover is incorrect, because you defined the problem incorrectly.

This section describes how to troubleshoot these main scenarios.

General Excel Error Messages

The following are the most common error messages that Solver can display after you click Tools ➤ Solver:

Active Document Is Not a Worksheet or Is Protected: This message is displayed when a protected worksheet is active when you click Tools ➤ Solver. To solve this problem, unprotect the worksheet.

Cannot Do This Command in Group Edit Mode: This message is displayed if multiple worksheets are selected when you click Tools ➤ Solver. To Solve this problem, select only one worksheet.

Cannot Do This Command in Data Entry Mode: This message is displayed if Excel is in data entry mode at the time you select the Solver menu choice. To solve this problem, exit data entry mode.

Solver Dialog Box Error Messages

Solver dialog box error messages usually appear because you attempt to define a particular setting for a model, and that setting is not allowed in a Solver dialog box. However, even after you define all of your settings and start Solver, it may stop running for several reasons. The error messages you may see in each of Solver's dialog boxes and how to address them are described in the following sections.

Solver Parameters Dialog Box

The Solver Parameters dialog box's most common error messages include the following:

Set Target Cell Contents Must Be a Formula: This message appears because the contents of the Set Target Cell box refer to a cell that doesn't contain a formula. To correct this problem, make sure that the Solver Parameter's dialog box's Set Target Cell box contains a reference to a cell that contains a formula.

Problem to Solve Not Specified: This message appears if you click the Solve button and you have not specified any adjustable cells in the By Changing Cells box, or if you have not specified a cell reference in the Set Target Cell box nor any constraints. To correct this problem, make sure that you have set, as a minimum, a cell reference in the Set Target Cell and By Changing Cells boxes.

By Changing Cells Must Be on the Active Sheet: This message appears if any of the cells referenced in the By Changing Cells box are not within the active worksheet. To correct this problem, redesign your model so that all the changing cells are all located on the active worksheet, and try running Solver again.

Cannot Guess By Changing Cells Without a Set Cell: This message appears if you click the Guess button without first referencing a cell in the Set Target Cell box. To correct this problem, click the Set Target Cell box and type or click the problem's target cell.

Cell Reference Box Is Empty or Contents Are Not Valid: This message appears in the Add/ Change Constraint dialog box if you click OK and the Cell Reference box is empty or contains something other than a valid cell reference. To solve this problem, correct the contents of the Cell Reference box to contain a valid cell reference, and then click OK again.

Constraint Must Be a Number, Simple Reference, or Formula with a Numeric Value: This message appears in the Add/Change Constraint dialog box if you click OK and the Constraint box is empty or doesn't contain a reference to a number, a cell reference, or a formula with a numeric value. To solve this problem, correct the contents of the Constraint box to reference a number, a cell reference, or a formula with a numeric value, and then click OK again.

Integer Constraint Cell Reference Must Include Only By Changing Cells: This message appears in the Add/Change Constraint dialog box if you click Int in the operator box, but the cells referenced in the Cell Reference box are not changing cells. To correct this problem, correct the contents of the Cell Reference box to reference changing cells.

Set Target Cell Must Be a Single Cell on the Active Sheet: This message appears if the reference in the Set Target Cell box contains something other than a single cell. To address this problem, correct the contents of the Set Target Cell box to reference a single cell on the active worksheet.

Set Target Cell Contents Must Be a Formula: This message appears if the cell referenced in the Set Target Cell box contains something other than a formula on the active worksheet. To address this problem, correct the contents of the Set Target Cell box to reference a cell on the active worksheet containing a formula that depends on changing cells on the active worksheet.

Set Target Cell Must Have Precedents Containing Numbers on the Active Sheet: This message appears if the cell referenced in the Set Target Cell box contains something other than a formula that depends on cells on the active sheet, some of which must be changing cells as referenced in the By Changing Cells box. To address this problem, correct the contents of the Set Target Cell box to reference a single cell on the active worksheet containing a formula that depends on changing cells on the active worksheet.

Too Many Adjustable Cells: This message appears if the number of cells referenced in the By Changing Cells box exceeds Solver's limits. To correct this problem, reduce the number of cells referenced in the By Changing Cells box.

Too Many Constraints: This message appears in the Add/Change Constraint dialog box if the number of cells in the Cell Reference edit box exceeds Solver's limits. To correct this problem, reduce the number of cells referenced in the Cell Reference box.

The Problem Is Too Large for Solver to Handle: This message appears when the total number of cells referenced in all constraints in the Subject to the Constraints list exceeds Solver's limits. To correct this problem, reduce the total number of cells referenced in the Subject to the Constraints list.

Unequal Number of Cells in Cell Reference and Constraint: This message appears in the Add/Change Constraint dialog box if the number of cells referenced in the Cell Reference box is not equal to the number of cells referenced in the Constraint box. To correct this problem, change the contents of the Cell Reference box or the Constraint box so that the number of cells in the Cell Reference box equals the number of cells referenced in the Constraint box.

Solver Options Dialog Box

The Solver Options dialog box's most common error messages include the following:

Max Time Must Be a Positive Number: This error message appears because the Max Time box's value is less than 1. To correct this problem, type a value of 1 or greater in the Max Time box.

Iterations Must Be a Positive Number: This error message appears because the Iterations box's value is less than 1. To correct this problem, type a whole number value of 1 or greater in the Iterations box.

Precision Must Be a Small Positive Number: This error message appears because the Precision box's value is less than or equal to 0 or greater than or equal to 1. To correct this problem, type a fractional number between 0 and 1 in the Precision box.

Integer Tolerance Must Be a Number Between 0 and 100: This error message appears because the Tolerance box's value is less than 0 or greater than 100. To correct this problem, type a value equal to or between 0 and 100 in the Tolerance box.

Convergence Must Be a Small Positive Number: This error message appears because the Convergence box's value is less than or equal to 0 or greater than or equal to 1. To correct this problem, type a fractional number between 0 and 1 in the Convergence box.

Solver Results Dialog Box

When Solver stops, regardless or whether it finds a solution, the Solver Results dialog box appears and displays a message. If this message is something other than that Solver found a solution, you can use the following troubleshooting tips based on the type of message displayed:

Solver Cannot Improve the Current Solution. All Constraints Are Satisfied: This message is displayed when Solver finds an approximate solution but cannot find a better set of values than those displayed. This is either because further accuracy is simply not achievable or the Precision setting is too low. To try to improve the current solution, try increasing the Solver Options dialog box's Precision setting to a larger number, and then running the problem again.

Stop Chosen When the Maximum Time Limit Was Reached: This message is displayed when Solver reaches the maximum amount of time specified without finding a satisfactory solution. To save the values that Solver found so far, as well as save future recalculation time, click either the Keep Solver Solution button or the Save Scenario button.

Stop Chosen When the Maximum Iteration Limit Was Reached: This message is displayed when Solver reaches the maximum number of iterations specified without finding a satisfactory solution. To save the values that Solver found and reduce future recalculation time, click the Keep Solver Solution button or the Save Scenario button. Increasing the number of iterations in the Solver Options dialog box's Iterations box might help Solver find a solution, but you should also consider examining the final values for insight into the problem.

The Set Target Cell Values Do Not Converge: This message is displayed when Solver cannot reach an upper or lower bound for the target cell, even though Solver may have met all of the model's constraints. This message usually appears because you may have omitted one or more constraints when you set up the model. To address this problem, check the current worksheet values to see how the solution is diverging, recheck the constraints, and then run Solver again.

Solver Could Not Find a Feasible Solution: This message is displayed when Solver cannot find a proposed solution that satisfies all of the model's constraints while still achieving the Solver Options dialog box's Precision setting. This message usually appears due to inconsistent constraints. To address this problem, examine the worksheet for a possible mistake in the constraints' formulas or in the choice of constraints.

Solver Stopped at User's Request: This message is displayed when you click the Show Trial Solution dialog box's Stop button, either when stepping through trial solutions or after pressing the Esc key to interrupt the solution process.

The Conditions for Assume Linear Model Are Not Satisfied: This message is displayed when the Solver Options dialog box's Assume Linear Model check box is selected, but Solver proposed values do not agree with a linear type of model. To check whether a problem is nonlinear, select the Solver Options dialog box's Use Automatic Scaling check box, and then run Solver again. If the same message reappears, clear the Assume Linear Model check box, and then run Solver again.

The Problem Is Too Large for Solver to Handle: This message is displayed when Solver determines that your model has too many decision variables or constraints. You will usually see this message only after you see a Too Many Adjustable Cells or Too Many Constraints message in the Solver Parameters dialog box. Solver can also display this message when there is an error in one of the cells on the right-hand side of a constraint. For example, if you have a constraint A1:A2 >= B1:B2, and B2 contains a #VALUE value, this message may appear.

Solver Encountered an Error Value in a Target or Constraint Cell: This message is displayed when Solver discovers an error value after its latest calculation. To address this message, find the target cell or constraint cell that contains the error, and do one of the following:

- Change the constraint cell's formula to return an appropriate numeric value.

- Make sure the constraints' names and formulas are valid in the Add Constraint dialog box for each constraint.

- Make sure you did not type Integer, Int, Binary, or Bin in any of the constraints' Add Constraint dialog boxes' Constraint boxes. Recall that to constrain a value to an integer, you just need to click Int in the operator list. Click Bin in the operator list to set a binary constraint.

There Is Not Enough Memory Available to Solve the Problem: This message is displayed when Excel cannot allocate enough computer memory to Solver. To address this message, close some files or programs, and then run Solver again.

Another Excel Instance Is Using SOLVER.DLL: This message is displayed when more than one Excel instance is running, and one of those Excel instances is already using Solver. Only one Excel instance can use Solver at a time. To address this message, stop Solver if it is running in any open Excel instance, or close all Excel instances that you are not currently using, and run Solver again.

Show Trial Solution Dialog Box

The Show Trial Solution dialog box's most common error message is the following:

The Scenario Manager Changing Cells Do Not Include All The Solver Changing Cells. Only The Scenario Manager Cell Values Will Be Saved: This message is displayed when you try to save the current changing cells' values as a scenario by clicking the Scenario button (this button is also available in the Solver Results dialog box), and you have previously used the Scenario Manager dialog box to define scenarios where the changing cells do not include all of the current changing cells. To solve this problem, modify the Scenario Manager dialog box's changing cells (by clicking Tools ➤ Scenarios), and then run Solver again.

General Troubleshooting Tips

If Solver does display a recommended solution, but you think that the solution is incorrect for some reason, try one or more of the following troubleshooting tips:

- Return to your model and check whether the selected target cell and the selected changing cells are relevant in the context of your problem.

- Examine the target cell's function definition and any constraints' function definitions for possible logic errors.

- Examine all of your constraints' definitions for possible logic errors.

- Make sure that all of your changing cells are somehow related to the target cell.

- Make sure that you have not omitted any important constraints from your model.

- Examine the Solver Options dialog box for any possible incorrect settings.

- Look for patterns in both the changing and nonchanging cells' data and form your own predictions about how what an optimal solution might look like. Then vary your cells' data and attempt to confirm your predictions on subsequent Solver runs.

- Look for named cell ranges that reference a worksheet that is not the current one. Although the reference is allowed, the actual cell value that is used is of the corresponding cell on the active sheet and not the one to which the reference is pointing.

Summary

In this chapter, you learned how to use Solver to help you find the desired exact value, minimum possible value, or maximum possible value for a single worksheet cell formula. You learned how to instruct Solver to use constraints to apply restrictions to the cell values that Solver can use to find your desired value, how to set Solver options, and how to generate and interpret Solver reports. To practice working with Solver, you completed three basic Try It exercises, as well as seven more involved exercises. Finally, you learned how to troubleshoot common problems with using Solver.

CHAPTER 5

■■■

Case Study: Using Excel What-If Tools

The preceding chapters have introduced four Excel what-if data analysis tools: Goal Seek, data tables, scenarios, and Solver. This chapter presents a case study demonstrating how a fictional running club, called the Ridge Running Cooperative, might use each of these what-if tools to produce reports and tools to assist runners. In the exercises in this chapter, you will use Goal Seek to forecast membership dues, data tables to forecast race paces, scenarios to forecast race-day cash flow, and Solver to forecast race-day finish times as well as pair up race relay teams.

About the Ridge Running Cooperative

Four years ago, residents of Red Hills Ridge, a city in the western part of the United States, formed a local running club named the Ridge Running Cooperative. Members of this not-for-profit cooperative volunteer their time at local running events in exchange for receiving special discounts on running apparel and nutritional supplements at several local athletic supply retail stores. Some of the club's members also serve as board members to oversee the cooperative's activities. At the end of every year after the club's operating expenses are paid, the board members distribute any remaining profits to track and field organizations in the local public school systems.

At the board's annual meeting toward the end of this year, board members have traditionally provided the following reports to all attending club members:

- A forecast of next year's annual membership dues income

- A forecast of next year's incoming cash flow from registrants for the annual Red Hills Ridge Labor Day race event

In addition, club members have asked the board's activities director to supply some special computer-based tools to assist runners. They would like tools to do the following:

- Forecast race paces

- Forecast race-day finish times

- Pair up relay race teams

The board's activities director has committed to producing these tools on compact disc (CD), which will be distributed to attending club members at the annual meeting.

The board's treasurer and activities director have decided to use the Excel what-if tools to produce these reports and tools. The following sections present a series of exercises to allow you to practice producing these reports and tools.

Use Goal Seek to Forecast Membership Dues

In this section, you will use Goal Seek to forecast next year's total club membership dues. This section's exercises are available in the Excel workbook named Ridge Running Exercises.xls, which is available for download from the Source Code area of the Apress web site (http://www.apress.com). These exercises' data is on the workbook's Membership Dues worksheet, as shown in Figure 5-1.

	A	B	C
1	New Individual Member Annual Dues	$30.00	
2	Renewing Individual Member Annual Dues	$25.00	
3	New Individual Member Lifetime Membership	$275.00	
4	New Family Annual Dues	$55.00	
5	Renewing Family Annual Dues	$45.00	
6	New Family Lifetime Membership	$400.00	
7			
8	New Individual Annual Members	95	$2,850.00
9	Renewing Individual Annual Members	135	$3,375.00
10	New Lifetime Individual Members	35	$9,625.00
11	New Annual Families	40	$2,200.00
12	Renewing Annual Families	65	$2,925.00
13	New Lifetime Families	20	$8,000.00
14			
15	Totals	390	$28,975.00

Figure 5-1. *The Membership Dues worksheet*

This worksheet contains the following information:

- New individual membership dues at a rate of $30.00 per year (cell B1, defined name NIMAD)

- Renewing individual membership dues at a rate of $25.00 per year (cell B2, defined name RIMAD)

- New individual lifetime membership dues at a one-time rate of $275.00 (cell B3, defined name NIMLM)

- New family membership dues at a rate of $55.00 per year (cell B4, defined name NFAD)

- Renewing family membership dues at a rate of $45.00 per year (cell B5, defined name RFAD)

- New family lifetime membership dues at a one-time rate of $400.00 (cell B6, defined name NFLM)

- The number of new annual individual memberships (cell B8, defined name NIAM)

- The number of renewing annual individual memberships (cell B9, defined name RIAM)

- The number of new individual lifetime memberships (cell B10, defined name NLIM)

- The number of new annual family memberships (cell B11, defined name NAF)

- The number of renewing annual family memberships (cell B12, defined name RAF)

- The number of new family lifetime memberships (cell B13, defined name NLM)

- The products of each dues level multiplied by the number of memberships at that level (cells C8 through C13)

- The total number of memberships (cell B15)

- The total membership dues (cell C15)

New Lifetime Family Club Membership Dues

Use Goal Seek to forecast how many new lifetime family club memberships are needed to achieve an overall club membership dues total of $30,000, assuming that all other club membership levels are constant.

1. Type the following values in the following cells:

    B8: **95**

    B9: **135**

    B10: **35**

    B11: **40**

    B12: **65**

2. Click Tools ➤ Goal Seek.

3. Click the Set Cell box, and then click or type cell **C15**.

4. Click the To Value box, and then type **30000**.

5. Click the By Changing Cell box, and then click or type cell **B13**.

6. Click OK, and then click OK again.

Compare your results to Figure 5-2. Note that the values are approximate due to the formatting and subsequent rounding of member and financial totals.

	A	B	C
1	New Individual Member Annual Dues	$30.00	
2	Renewing Individual Member Annual Dues	$25.00	
3	New Individual Member Lifetime Membership	$275.00	
4	New Family Annual Dues	$55.00	
5	Renewing Family Annual Dues	$45.00	
6	New Family Lifetime Membership	$400.00	
7			
8	New Individual Annual Members	95	$2,850.00
9	Renewing Individual Annual Members	135	$3,375.00
10	New Lifetime Individual Members	35	$9,625.00
11	New Annual Families	40	$2,200.00
12	Renewing Annual Families	65	$2,925.00
13	New Lifetime Families	(23)	$9,025.00
14			
15	Totals	393	($30,000.00)

Figure 5-2. *Results of goal seeking for new lifetime family club memberships*

New Annual Family Club Memberships

Use Goal Seek to forecast how many new annual family club memberships are needed to achieve a new annual family club membership total of $3,000, assuming that all other club membership levels from the previous exercise are constant.

1. Using the results from the previous exercise, click Tools ➤ Goal Seek.

2. Click the Set Cell box, and then click or type cell **C11**.

3. Click the To Value box, and then type **3000**.

4. Click the By Changing Cell box, and then click or type cell **B11**.

5. Click OK, and then click OK again.

Compare your results to Figure 5-3.

	A	B	C
1	New Individual Member Annual Dues	$30.00	
2	Renewing Individual Member Annual Dues	$25.00	
3	New Individual Member Lifetime Membership	$275.00	
4	New Family Annual Dues	$55.00	
5	Renewing Family Annual Dues	$45.00	
6	New Family Lifetime Membership	$400.00	
7			
8	New Individual Annual Members	95	$2,850.00
9	Renewing Individual Annual Members	135	$3,375.00
10	New Lifetime Individual Members	35	$9,625.00
11	New Annual Families	55	$3,000.00
12	Renewing Annual Families	65	$2,925.00
13	New Lifetime Families	23	$9,025.00
14			
15	Totals	407	$30,800.00

Figure 5-3. *Results of goal seeking for new annual family club memberships*

Use Data Tables to Forecast Race Paces

In this section, you will use one-variable and two-variable data tables to forecast various race paces. Simply defined, a *race pace* is the average time for a given distance between two points. Paces are usually expressed as the average number of minutes it takes to run an average kilometer or mile. So, if you run a 10-minute-per-mile pace, this means it takes you an average of 10 minutes to run an average mile.

Time for a Single Race Pace

The first exercise in this section uses a one-variable data table to forecast the average amount of time it would take to run various distances at a single race pace. This exercise's data is on the Ridge Running Exercises.xls workbook's Race Paces 1 worksheet, as shown in Figure 5-4.

This worksheet contains the following information:

- Column A (cells A4 through A17) displays the number of miles, 1 through 13.1 (the length of a half-marathon race is 13.1 miles).

- Column B (cells B4 through B17) will display the average number of minutes to run the various distances at the race pace in cell B3.

Use a one-variable data table to calculate the average amount of time it would take to run from 1 through 13.1 miles at an 8.5-minute-per-mile pace.

	A	B
1		1
2		8.5
3		8.5
4	1	
5	2	
6	3	
7	4	
8	5	
9	6	
10	7	
11	8	
12	9	
13	10	
14	11	
15	12	
16	13	
17	13.1	

Figure 5-4. *The blank one-variable race paces worksheet*

1. Select cells A3 through B17.

2. Click Data ➤ Table.

3. Click Column Input Cell.

4. Click cell B1.

5. Click OK.

Compare your results to Figure 5-5.

Tip You can change the race pace variable (in cell B2) in one location and have those changes immediately reflected in the times for each distance. For example, try changing the value of cell B2 to the number 9 and see how the values in cells B4 to B17 change accordingly.

	A	B
1		1
2		8.5
3		8.5
4	1	8.5
5	2	17
6	3	25.5
7	4	34
8	5	42.5
9	6	51
10	7	59.5
11	8	68
12	9	76.5
13	10	85
14	11	93.5
15	12	102
16	13	110.5
17	13.1	111.35

Figure 5-5. *Results of calculating race times using a one-variable data table*

Time for Multiple Race Paces

The second exercise in this section uses a two-variable data table to forecast the average amount of time it would take to run various distances at several race paces. This exercise's data is on the Ridge Running Exercises.xls workbook's Race Paces 2 worksheet, as shown in Figure 5-6.

	A	B	C	D	E	F	G	H	I	J
1	1									
2	5									
3	5	5	5.5	6	6.5	7	7.5	8	8.5	9
4	1									
5	2									
6	3									
7	4									
8	5									
9	6									
10	7									
11	8									
12	9									
13	10									
14	11									
15	12									
16	13									
17	13.1									

Figure 5-6. *The blank two-variable race paces worksheet*

This worksheet contains the following information:

- Column A (cells A4 through A17) is the same as the Race Paces 1 worksheet, displaying the number of miles, 1 through 13.1.

- Columns B through J (cells B4 through J17) will display the average number of minutes to run the various distances at the race paces in cells B3 through J3.

Use a two-variable data table to calculate the average amount of time it would take to run from 1 through 13.1 miles at 5-minute-per-mile through 9-minute-per-mile paces, in half-minute increments.

1. Select cells A3 through J17.

2. Click Data ➤ Table.

3. Click Row Input Cell.

4. Click cell A2.

5. Click Column Input Cell.

6. Click cell A1.

7. Click OK.

Compare your results to Figure 5-7.

	A	B	C	D	E	F	G	H	I	J
1	1									
2	5									
3	5	5	5.5	6	6.5	7	7.5	8	8.5	9
4	1	5	5.5	6	6.5	7	7.5	8	8.5	9
5	2	10	11	12	13	14	15	16	17	18
6	3	15	16.5	18	19.5	21	22.5	24	25.5	27
7	4	20	22	24	26	28	30	32	34	36
8	5	25	27.5	30	32.5	35	37.5	40	42.5	45
9	6	30	33	36	39	42	45	48	51	54
10	7	35	38.5	42	45.5	49	52.5	56	59.5	63
11	8	40	44	48	52	56	60	64	68	72
12	9	45	49.5	54	58.5	63	67.5	72	76.5	81
13	10	50	55	60	65	70	75	80	85	90
14	11	55	60.5	66	71.5	77	82.5	88	93.5	99
15	12	60	66	72	78	84	90	96	102	108
16	13	65	71.5	78	84.5	91	97.5	104	110.5	117
17	13.1	65.5	72.05	78.6	85.15	91.7	98.25	104.8	111.35	117.9

Figure 5-7. *Results of calculating race times using a two-variable data table*

■Tip You can use a Visual Basic for Applications (VBA) macro included in this workbook to quickly convert minutes in decimal format to hour/minute/second (hh:mm:ss) format. To do this, click a single cell containing the number of minutes (for example, 111.35), press Ctrl+Shift+M, and look at the status bar (for example, 111.35 minutes = 1:51:21). You can use another VBA macro included in this workbook to reset the value from the status bar. To do this, press Ctrl+Shift+R. To examine the macros' code, click Tools ➤ Macro ➤ Macros, click ThisWorkbook.ConvertMinutesToHHMMSS or ThisWorkbook.ResetStatusBar, and then click the Edit button.

Use Scenarios to Forecast Race-Day Cash Flow

In this section, you will use scenarios to forecast next year's projected incoming cash flow from registrants for the annual Red Hills Ridge Labor Day Race event.

The data for this set of exercises is on the Ridge Running Exercises.xls workbook's Race Day Cash Flow worksheet, as shown in Figure 5-8.

	A	B	C	D	E	F
1		2K Kids Dash	5K Run/Walk	10K Run/Walk	Half Marathon Run/Walk	Marathon Run/Walk
2	Early Bird Registration Fee	$8.00	$15.00	$20.00	$60.00	$80.00
3	Regular Registration Fee	$10.00	$18.00	$25.00	$70.00	$90.00
4	Day-Of-Race Registration Fee	$15.00	$20.00	$30.00	$85.00	$115.00
5						
6	Early Bird Registrants	1	1	1	1	1
7	Regular Registrants	1	1	1	1	1
8	Day-Of-Race Registrants	1	1	1	1	1
9						
10	Subtotals	$33.00	$53.00	$75.00	$215.00	$285.00
11	Grand Total	$661.00				

Figure 5-8. *The incoming cash flow worksheet for Red Hills Ridge Half Marathon event registrants*

This worksheet contains the following information:

- The early bird registration fee for the 2-kilometer kids dash (cell B2, defined name EBRF2K)

- The early bird registration fee for the 5-kilometer run/walk race (cell C2, defined name EBRF5K)

- The early bird registration fee for the 10-kilometer run/walk race (cell D2, defined name EBRF10K)

- The early bird registration fee for the half marathon run/walk race (cell E2, defined name EBRFHM)

- The early bird registration fee for the marathon run/walk race (cell F2, defined name EBRFM)

- The regular registration fee for the 2-kilometer kids dash (cell B3, defined name RRF2K)

- The regular registration fee for the 5-kilometer run/walk race (cell C3, defined name RRF5K)

- The regular registration fee for the 10-kilometer run/walk race (cell D3, defined name RRF10K)

- The regular registration fee for the half marathon run/walk race (cell E3, defined name RRFHM)

- The regular registration fee for the marathon run/walk race (cell F3, defined name RRFM)

- The day-of-race registration fee for the 2-kilometer kids dash (cell B4, defined name DORF2K)

- The day-of-race registration fee for the 5-kilometer run/walk race (cell C4, defined name DORF5K)

- The day-of-race registration fee for the 10-kilometer run/walk race (cell D4, defined name DORF10K)

- The day-of-race registration fee for the half marathon run/walk race (cell E4, defined name DORFHM)

- The day-of-race registration fee for the marathon run/walk race (cell F4, defined name DORFM)

- The number of early bird registrants for the 2-kilometer kids dash (cell B6, defined name EB2K)

- The number of early bird registrants for the 5-kilometer run/walk race (cell C6, defined name EB5K)

- The number of early bird registrants for the 10-kilometer run/walk race (cell D6, defined name EB10K)

- The number of early bird registrants for the half marathon run/walk race (cell E6, defined name EBHM)

- The number of early bird registrants for the marathon run/walk race (cell F6, defined name EBM)

- The number of regular registrants for the 2-kilometer kids dash (cell B7, defined name RR2K)

- The number of regular registrants for the 5-kilometer run/walk race (cell C7, defined name RR5K)

- The number of regular registrants for the 10-kilometer run/walk race (cell D7, defined name RR10K)

- The number of regular registrants for the half marathon run/walk race (cell E7, defined name RRHM)

- The number of regular registrants for the marathon run/walk race (cell F7, defined name RRM)

- The number of day-of-race registrants for the 2-kilometer kids dash (cell B8, defined name DOR2K)

- The number of day-of-race registrants for the 5-kilometer run/walk race (cell C8, defined name DOR5K)

- The number of day-of-race registrants for the 10-kilometer run/walk race (cell D8, defined name DOR10K)

- The number of day-of-race registrants for the half marathon run/walk race (cell E8, defined name DORHM)

- The number of day-of-race registrants for the marathon run/walk race (cell F8, defined name DORM)

- Subtotals for 2-kilometer, 5-kilometer, 10-kilometer, half marathon, and marathon registration fees (cells B10 through F10)

- The grand total for all registration fees (cell B11)

Cash Flow for a Rainy Weather Race Day

Create a scenario to forecast next year's projected incoming cash flow from registrants based on rainy weather the day of the race.

1. Select cells B6 through F8.

2. Click Tools ➤ Scenarios.

3. Click Add.

4. In the Scenario Name box, type **Rainy Weather Race Day Scenario**.

5. Click OK.

6. Type these values in the following cells:

        EB2K: **55**

        EB5K: **125**

        EB10K: **110**

        EBHM: **90**

        EBM: **50**

        RR2K: **95**

        RR5K: **200**

RR10K: **180**

RRHM: **120**

RRM: **75**

DOR2K: **50**

DOR5K: **100**

DOR10K: **95**

DORHM: **75**

DORM: **40**

7. Click OK.

8. Click Show.

9. Click Close.

Compare your results to Figure 5-9.

	A	B	C	D	E	F
1		2K Kids Dash	5K Run/Walk	10K Run/Walk	Half Marathon Run/Walk	Marathon Run/Walk
2	Early Bird Registration Fee	$8.00	$15.00	$20.00	$60.00	$80.00
3	Regular Registration Fee	$10.00	$18.00	$25.00	$70.00	$90.00
4	Day-Of-Race Registration Fee	$15.00	$20.00	$30.00	$85.00	$115.00
5						
6	Early Bird Registrants	55	125	110	90	50
7	Regular Registrants	95	200	180	120	75
8	Day-Of-Race Registrants	50	100	95	75	40
9						
10	Subtotals	$2,140.00	$7,475.00	$9,550.00	$20,175.00	$15,350.00
11	Grand Total	$54,690.00				

Figure 5-9. *Results of using scenarios to forecast cash flow for a rainy weather race day*

Cash Flow for a Normal Weather Race Day

Create a scenario to forecast next year's projected incoming cash flow from registrants based on normal weather the day of the race. Note that the only change between this scenario and the previous scenario is the number of day-of-race registrants, which is expected to be higher for normal race-day weather than for rainy race-day weather.

1. Select cells B6 through F8.

2. Click Tools ➤ Scenarios.

3. Click Add.

4. In the Scenario Name box, type **Normal Weather Race Day Scenario**.

5. Click OK.

6. Change the values in only the following cells:

DOR2K: **75**

DOR5K: **130**

DOR10K: **120**

DORHM: **100**

DORM: **55**

7. Click OK.

8. Click Show.

9. Click Close.

Compare your results to Figure 5-10.

	A	B	C	D	E	F
1		2K Kids Dash	5K Run/Walk	10K Run/Walk	Half Marathon Run/Walk	Marathon Run/Walk
2	Early Bird Registration Fee	$8.00	$15.00	$20.00	$60.00	$80.00
3	Regular Registration Fee	$10.00	$18.00	$25.00	$70.00	$90.00
4	Day-Of-Race Registration Fee	$15.00	$20.00	$30.00	$85.00	$115.00
5						
6	Early Bird Registrants	55	125	110	90	50
7	Regular Registrants	95	200	180	120	75
8	Day-Of-Race Registrants	75	130	120	100	55
9						
10	Subtotals	$2,515.00	$8,075.00	$10,300.00	$22,300.00	$17,075.00
11	Grand Total	$60,265.00				

Figure 5-10. *Results of using scenarios to forecast cash flow for a normal weather race day*

Cash Flow for a Perfect Weather Race Day

Create a scenario to forecast next year's projected incoming cash flow from registrants based on perfect weather the day of the race. Note that the only change between this scenario and the previous two scenarios is the number of day-of-race registrants, which is expected to be higher for perfect race-day weather than for rainy and normal race-day weather.

1. Select cells B6 through F8.

2. Click Tools ➤ Scenarios.

3. Click Add.

4. In the Scenario Name box, type **Perfect Weather Race Day Scenario**.

5. Click OK.

6. Change the values in only the following cells:

DOR2K: **110**

DOR5K: **170**

DOR10K: **150**

DORHM: **110**

DORM: **70**

7. Click OK.

8. Click Show.

9. Click Close.

Compare your results to Figure 5-11.

	A	B	C	D	E	F
1		2K Kids Dash	5K Run/Walk	10K Run/Walk	Half Marathon Run/Walk	Marathon Run/Walk
2	Early Bird Registration Fee	$8.00	$15.00	$20.00	$60.00	$80.00
3	Regular Registration Fee	$10.00	$18.00	$25.00	$70.00	$90.00
4	Day-Of-Race Registration Fee	$15.00	$20.00	$30.00	$85.00	$115.00
5						
6	Early Bird Registrants	55	125	110	90	50
7	Regular Registrants	95	200	180	120	75
8	Day-Of-Race Registrants	110	170	150	110	70
9						
10	Subtotals	$3,040.00	$8,875.00	$11,200.00	$23,150.00	$18,800.00
11	Grand Total	$65,065.00				

Figure 5-11. *Results of using scenarios to forecast cash flow for a perfect weather race day*

Report to Display Race-Day Cash-Flow Forecasts Side by Side

Create a scenario summary report to display the previous three race-day cash-flow forecasts next to each other on a new worksheet.

1. Click Tools ➤ Scenarios.

2. Click Summary.

3. Click the Scenario Summary option.

4. Click the Result Cells box, and then select cells B10 through F10 and cell B11.

5. Click OK.

Compare your results to Figure 5-12.

	B	C	D	G	H
2	**Scenario Summary**				
3			Current Values:	Perfect Weather Race Day Scenario	Normal Weather Race Day Scenario
5	**Changing Cells:**				
6	EB2K		55	55	55
7	EB5K		125	125	125
19	DORHM		110	110	100
20	DORM		70	70	55
21	**Result Cells:**				
22	Fees2K	$3,040.00		$3,040.00	$2,515.00
23	Fees5K	$8,875.00		$8,875.00	$8,075.00
24	Fees10K	$11,200.00		$11,200.00	$10,300.00
25	FeesHalfM	$23,150.00		$23,150.00	$22,300.00
26	FeesM	$18,800.00		$18,800.00	$17,075.00
27	TotalFees	$65,065.00		$65,065.00	$60,265.00

Figure 5-12. *Results of creating a scenario summary report to display several race-day cash-flow forecasts side by side*

Report to Display Race-Day Cash-Flow Forecasts in PivotTable Format

Create a scenario PivotTable report to display the previous three race-day cash-flow forecasts in a PivotTable. To begin, click the Race Day Cash Flow worksheet tab.

1. Click Tools ➤ Scenarios.

2. Click Summary.

3. Click the Scenario PivotTable Report option.

4. Click the Result Cells box, and then select cells B10 through F10 and cell B11.

5. Click OK.

Compare your results to Figure 5-13.

	A	B	C	D	E	F	G
1	$B$6:$F$8 by	(All) ▾					
2							
3		Result Cells ▾					
4	$B$6:$F$8 ▾	Fees2K	Fees5K	Fees10K	FeesHalfM	FeesM	TotalFees
5	Normal Weather Race Day Scenario	2515	8075	10300	22300	17075	60265
6	Original Values	33	53	75	215	285	661
7	Perfect Weather Race Day Scenario	3040	8875	11200	23150	18800	65065
8	Rainy Weather Race Day Scenario	2140	7475	9550	20175	15350	54690

Figure 5-13. *Results of creating a scenario PivotTable report to display several race-day cash-flow forecasts in PivotTable format*

Now, clean up the PivotTable's appearance and display format.

1. Right-click cell A1 (the cell containing $B$6:$F$8 by) and click Hide.

2. Right-click cell A4 (the cell containing $B$6:$F$8) and click Field Settings.

3. Click the Name box, type **Scenario**, and click OK.

4. Right-click cell B5 (2K Kids Dash Fees) and click Field Settings.

5. Click Number.

6. Click Currency.

7. Click OK, and then click OK again.

8. Repeat steps 4 through 7 for cells C5, D5, E5, F5, and G5.

Compare your results to Figure 5-14.

	A	B	C	D	E	F	G
1							
2							
3		Result Cells ▾					
4	Scenario ▾	Fees2K	Fees5K	Fees10K	FeesHalfM	FeesM	TotalFees
5	Normal Weather Race Day Scenario	$2,515.00	$8,075.00	$10,300.00	$22,300.00	$17,075.00	$60,265.00
6	Original Values	$33.00	$53.00	$75.00	$215.00	$285.00	$661.00
7	Perfect Weather Race Day Scenario	$3,040.00	$8,875.00	$11,200.00	$23,150.00	$18,800.00	$65,065.00
8	Rainy Weather Race Day Scenario	$2,140.00	$7,475.00	$9,550.00	$20,175.00	$15,350.00	$54,690.00

Figure 5-14. *Results of cleaning up the PivotTable's appearance and display format*

Use Solver to Forecast Race-Day Finish Times

In this section, you will use Solver to forecast race-day finish times using three primary timing methods:

- Given a distance in kilometers or miles and a target pace per kilometer or mile in minutes, you can forecast how many minutes it will take to cover that distance.

- Given a distance in kilometers or miles and how long it took for a runner to cover that distance in minutes, you can forecast a target pace per kilometer or mile in minutes.

- Given a distance in kilometers or miles, your target pace per kilometer or mile in minutes, and a pacer's total number of minutes to cover that distance, you can forecast how many total minutes faster or slower a runner will be from the pacer's time, as well a how many minutes faster or slower a runner will be from the pacer's target pace per kilometer or mile in minutes.

■**Note** A *pacer* is someone who runs in a race at a set number of minutes per kilometer or mile. Theoretically, if you run alongside this person, you should be able to finish the race in the exact amount of time as set by the pacer. A pacer is typically a race volunteer who has a sign pinned to his back that reads something like "Run with me to finish in 2 hours and 30 minutes" or simply "Pace 2:30:00." In bigger races, there are usually several pacers at various speeds running throughout the race course.

The data for this set of exercises is on the Ridge Running Exercises.xls workbook's Finish Times worksheet, as shown in Figure 5-15.

	A	B
1	*Using Distance and Target Pace*	
2	Total Distance (km/Miles)	13.1
3	Target Minutes Per Km/Mile	8.65
4	Target Finish Time (Minutes)	113.315
5		
6	*Using Distance and Elapsed Time*	
7	Total Distance (km/Miles)	13.1
8	Total Elapsed Time (Minutes)	126
9	Average Minutes Per Km/Mile	9.618321
10		
11	*Using a Pacer*	
12	Total Distance (km/Miles)	13.1
13	Your Minutes Per Km/Mile	10
14	Pacer's Target Finish Time (Minutes)	120
15	Difference From Pacer's Time (Minutes)	11
16	Difference From Pacer's Time (Minutes Per Km/Mile)	0.839695

Figure 5-15. *The race-day finish times forecasting worksheet*

This worksheet contains the following information:

- For forecasting elapsed time given total distance and target pace, the total distance is specified in cell B2, the target pace is specified in cell B3, and the elapsed time is displayed in cell B4.

- For forecasting target pace given total distance and elapsed time, the total distance is specified in cell B7, the elapsed time is specified in cell B8, and the target pace is displayed in cell B9.

- For forecasting the difference in elapsed time and target pace from a pacer, the total distance is specified in cell B12, your target pace is specified in cell B13, the pacer's elapsed time is specified in cell B14, your difference in elapsed time from the pacer is displayed in cell B15, and your difference in target pace from the pacer is displayed in cell B16.

Race-Day Finish Times with Distance and Target Pace

Use Solver along with cells B2 through B4 to forecast the maximum number of miles you could run in two hours given a target pace of 9.5 minutes per mile.

1. Click Tools ➤ Solver.

2. Click Reset All, and then click OK.

3. Click the Set Target Cell box, and then click cell B4.

4. Click the Value Of option, and then type **120** in the Value Of box.

5. Click the By Changing Cells box, and then select cells B2 and B3.

6. Click Add.

7. Click the Cell Reference box, and then click cell B3.

8. In the operator list, click =.

9. Click the Constraint box, and then type **9.5**.

10. Click OK.

11. Click Solve, and then click OK.

Compare your results to Figure 5-16.

	A	B
1	*Using Distance and Target Pace*	
2	Total Distance (km/Miles)	12.63158
3	Target Minutes Per Km/Mile	9.5
4	Target Finish Time (Minutes)	120

Figure 5-16. *Using Solver to forecast the maximum number of miles you could run in two hours given a target pace of 9.5 minutes per mile*

Now, save this problem as a model.

1. Click Tools ➤ Solver.

2. You will see that the Solver Parameters dialog box retained the settings from the previous exercise. Click Options.

3. Click Save Model.

4. Click cell D19, and then click OK.

5. Click OK to return to the Solver Parameters dialog box, and then click Close.

Finally, load the previously saved model.

1. Change the values in cells B2 and B3, so that you can see the numbers change when you load a saved model (for example, type **10** in cell B2 and **9** in cell B3).

2. Click Tools ➤ Solver.

3. Click Reset All, and then click OK.

4. Click Options.

5. Click Load Model.

6. Select cells D19 through D22, and then click OK.

7. Click OK to return to the Solver Parameters dialog box.

8. Click Solve, and then click OK.

Compare your results to Figure 5-16 again.

Race-Day Finish Times with Distance and Elapsed Time

Use Solver along with cells B7 through B9 to forecast the time it would take to complete a marathon (26.2 miles) at a pace of 10.5 minutes per mile.

1. Click Tools ➤ Solver.

2. Click Reset All, and then click OK.

3. Click the Set Target Cell box, and then click cell B9.

4. Click the Value Of option, and then type **10.5** in the Value Of box.

5. Click the By Changing Cells box, and then select cells B7 and B8.

6. Click Add.

7. Click the Cell Reference box, and then click cell B7.

8. In the operator list, click =.

9. Click the Constraint box, and then type **26.2**.

10. Click OK.

11. Click Solve, and then click OK.

Compare your results to Figure 5-17.

6	*Using Distance and Elapsed Time*	
7	Total Distance (km/Miles)	26.2
8	Total Elapsed Time (Minutes)	275.1
9	Average Minutes Per Km/Mile	10.5

Figure 5-17. *Using Solver to forecast the time it would take to complete a marathon at a pace of 10.5 minutes per mile*

Race-Day Finish Times with a Pacer

Use Solver along with cells B12 through B16 to forecast your target pace per mile given a distance of 6.2 miles (10 kilometers), a pacer's target finish time of 52 minutes, and a desired target pace per mile of 15 seconds faster than the pacer.

1. Click Tools ➤ Solver.

2. Click Reset All, and then click OK.

3. Click the Set Target Cell box, and then click cell B16.

4. Click the Value Of option, and then type **0.25** in the Value Of box.

5. Click the By Changing Cells box, and then select cells B12 through B14.

6. Click Add.

7. Click the Cell Reference box, and then click cell B12.

8. In the operator list, click =.

9. Click the Constraint box, and then type **6.2**.

10. Click Add.

11. Click the Cell Reference box, and then click cell B14.

12. In the operator list, click =.

13. Click the Constraint box, and then type **52**.

14. Click OK.

15. Click Solve, and then click OK.

    Compare your results to Figure 5-18.

11	*Using a Pacer*	
12	Total Distance (km/Miles)	6.2
13	Your Minutes Per Km/Mile	8.637097
14	Pacer's Target Finish Time (Minutes)	52
15	Difference From Pacer's Time (Minutes)	1.55
16	Difference From Pacer's Time (Minutes Per Km/Mile)	0.25

Figure 5-18. *Using Solver to forecast your target pace per mile given a distance of 10 kilometers, a pacer's target finish time of 52 minutes, and a desired target pace per mile of 15 seconds (0.25 minute) faster than the pacer*

Use Solver to Pair Up Race Relay Teams

In this section, you will use Solver to determine whether a particular runner would be a good candidate for a race relay team, given factors such as total race distance, number of runners on the relay team, the target elapsed finish time, and so on.

This exercise's data is on the Ridge Running Exercises.xls workbook's Relay Teams worksheet, as shown in Figure 5-19.

	A	B
1		
2	Total Distance (km/Miles)	26.2
3	Total Number of Racers	3
4	Target Total Finish Time (Minutes)	240
5	Total Distance (km/Miles) Per Racer	8.733333
6	Average Minutes Per Km/Mile	9.160305
7	Total Minutes Per Racer	80
8		
9	Your Average Minutes Per Km/Mile	9
10	Qualify for This Relay Team?	Yes

Figure 5-19. *The relay teams pairing worksheet*

This worksheet contains the following information:

- The race's total distance, in kilometers or miles, is provided in cell B2.

- The number of racers on the race relay team is provided in cell B3.

- The target elapsed race finish time, in minutes, is provided in cell B4.

- The distance, in kilometers or miles, that each race relay team member will run is provided in cell B5.

- The pace in minutes per kilometer or mile that each race relay team member needs to run to meet or beat the target elapsed race finish for the given distance is provided in cell B6.

- The elapsed time per race relay team member is provided in cell B7.

- You enter your projected pace in minutes per kilometer or mile in cell B9.

- Cell B10 displays whether you are a good candidate for this particular relay team.

Use Solver to determine whether you are a good candidate for a five-person race relay team running a distance of 62 miles (100 kilometers), with no team member running for more than 1.5 hours, assuming your average pace per mile is 8.75 minutes.

1. Click Tools ➤ Solver.

2. Click Reset All, and then click OK.

3. Click the Set Target Cell box, and then click cell B7.

4. Click the Value Of option, and then type **90** in the Value Of box.

5. Click the By Changing Cells box, and then select cells B2, B3, B4, and B9.

6. Click Add.

7. Click the Cell Reference box, and then click cell B2.

8. In the operator list, click =.

9. Click the Constraint box, and then type **62**.

10. Click Add.

11. Click the Cell Reference box, and then click cell B3.

12. In the operator list, click =.

13. Click the Constraint box, and then type **5**.

14. Click Add.

15. Click the Cell Reference box, and then click cell B9.

16. In the operator list, click =.

17. Click the Constraint box, and then type **8.75**.

18. Click OK.

19. Click Solve, and then click OK.

Compare your results to Figure 5-20.

	A	B
1		
2	Total Distance (km/Miles)	62
3	Total Number of Racers	5
4	Target Total Finish Time (Minutes)	450
5	Total Distance (km/Miles) Per Racer	12.4
6	Average Minutes Per Km/Mile	7.258065
7	Total Minutes Per Racer	90
8		
9	Your Average Minutes Per Km/Mile	8.75
10	Qualify for This Relay Team?	No

Figure 5-20. *Using Solver to determine whether you are a good candidate for a five-person race relay team running a distance of 62 miles, with no team member running for more than 1.5 hours, assuming your average pace per mile is 8.75 minutes*

Summary

In this chapter, you completed several exercises that demonstrated in case-study format how to do the following:

- Use Goal Seek to forecast a running club's membership dues.

- Use one-variable and two-variable data tables to forecast race paces.

- Use scenarios to forecast race-day cash flow.

- Use Solver to forecast race-day finish times and pair up race relay teams.

APPENDIX A

◼◼◼

Excel What-If Tools Quick Start

This appendix provides a brief introduction to the Excel what-if data analysis tools: Goal Seek, data tables, scenarios, and Solver. Each introduction is accompanied by a simple example.

Using Goal Seek

Goal Seek is a simple, easy-to-use, timesaving tool that enables you to calculate a formula's input value when you want to work backwards from the formula's answer. You use Goal Seek when you want to find a specific value for a single worksheet cell by adjusting the value of one other worksheet cell. When you know the desired result of a single formula but not the input value the formula needs to determine the result, Goal Seek is a good tool to use.

Goal Seek Procedure

To use Goal Seek in Excel, follow these steps:

1. Click Tools ➤ Goal Seek.

2. In the Set Cell box, click or type the reference to the single worksheet cell that contains the formula for which you want to find a specific result.

3. In the To Value box, type the result that you want to find.

4. In the By Changing Value box, click or type the reference to single worksheet cell that contains the value you want to change. This cell must be referenced by the formula in the cell referenced in the Set Cell box.

5. Click OK.

Goal Seek Example

Given the sample data in Figure A-1, use Goal Seek to calculate the number of ounces in three liters.

	A	B	C
1	Ounces	101.42	
2	Gallons	0.792344	← CONVERT(B1, "oz", "gal")
3	Liters	3	← CONVERT(B2, "gal", "lt")

Figure A-1. *Goal Seek sample data*

1. Click Tools ➤ Goal Seek.

2. Click the Set Cell box, and then click cell B3.

3. Click the To Value box, and then type **3**.

4. Click the By Changing Cell box, and then click cell B1.

5. Click OK.

Answer: There are 101.42 ounces in three liters.

Using Data Tables

Data tables are a handy way to display the results of multiple-formula calculations in an at-a-glance lookup format. A data table is a collection of cells that displays how changing values in worksheet formulas affects the results of those formulas. Data tables provide a convenient way to calculate, display, and compare multiple outcomes of a given formula in a single operation. You use data tables when you want to provide a convenient way to represent in a table-like format the results of running several iterations of a formula using various inputs to that formula.

Excel has two types of data tables: *one-variable data tables* and *two-variable data tables*. One-variable data tables have only one input value, while two-variable data tables have two input values.

Data Table Procedure

To create a one-variable data table in Excel, follow these steps:

1. Type the list of values that you want to substitute in the input cell's value either down one column or across one row.

2. Do one of the following:

   - If the list of values is down one column, type the formula in the row above the first value and one cell to the right of the column of values.

   - If the list of values is across one row, type the formula in the column to the left of the first value and one cell below the row of values.

3. Select the range of cells that contains the formulas and values that you want to substitute.

4. Click Data ➤ Table.

5. Do one of the following:

   - If the list of values is down one column, click or type the cell reference for the input cell in the Column Input Cell box.

   - If the list of values is across one row, click or type the cell reference for the input cell in the Row Input Cell box.

6. Click OK.

To create a two-variable data table in Excel, follow these steps:

1. In a cell on the worksheet, enter the formula that refers to the two input cells.

2. Type one list of input values in the same column, below the formula.

3. Type the second list in the same row, to the right of the formula.

4. Select the range of cells that contains the formula and both the row and column of values.

5. Click Data ➤ Table.

6. In the Row Input Cell box, click or type the reference to the input cell for the input values in the row.

7. In the Column Input Cell box, click or type the reference to the input cell for the input values in the column.

8. Click OK.

Data Table Examples

Given the sample data in Figure A-2, create a one-variable data table to display the number of feet in a specified number of miles.

	A	B	C
1		1	
2		5280	← CONVERT(B1, "mi", "ft")
3	1		
4	2		
5	3		
6	4		
7	5		
8	Miles	Feet	

Figure A-2. *One-variable data table with starting sample data*

1. Select cells A2 through B7.

2. Click Data ➤ Table.

3. Click the Column Input Cell box, and then click cell B1.

4. Click OK. Compare your results with Figure A-3.

	A	B	C
1		1	
2		5280	← CONVERT(B1, "mi", "ft")
3	1	5280	
4	2	10560	
5	3	15840	
6	4	21120	
7	5	26400	
8	Miles	Feet	

Figure A-3. *Completed one-variable data table*

Given the sample data in Figure A-4, create a two-variable data table to display the total area given a specified length and width of the area.

	A	B	C	D	E	F	G
1	3						
2	9	↖ A1*A2					
3	27	1	2	3	4	5	Width
4	1						
5	2						
6	3						
7	4						
8	5						
9	Length						

Figure A-4. *Two-variable data table with starting sample data*

1. Select cells A3 through F8.

2. Click Data ➤ Table.

3. Click the Row Input Cell box, and then click cell A2.

4. Click the Column Input Cell box, and then click cell A1.

5. Click OK. Compare your results with Figure A-5.

	A	B	C	D	E	F	G
1	3						
2	9	↖ A1*A2					
3	27	1	2	3	4	5	Width
4	1	1	2	3	4	5	
5	2	2	4	6	8	10	
6	3	3	6	9	12	15	
7	4	4	8	12	16	20	
8	5	5	10	15	20	25	
9	Length						

Figure A-5. *Completed two-variable data table*

Using Scenarios

A scenario is a set of worksheet cell values and formulas that Excel saves as a group. You can then have Excel automatically substitute that set for another group of cell values and formulas in a worksheet. You use scenarios to forecast the outcome of a particular set of worksheet cell values and formulas that refer to those cell values.

Scenario Procedure

To create a scenario in Excel, follow these steps:

1. Click Tools ➤ Scenarios.

2. Click Add.

3. In the Scenario Name box, type a name for the scenario.

4. In the Changing Cells box, click or type the reference for the worksheet cells that you want to change.

5. Click OK.

6. In the Scenario Values dialog box, type the values you want for the changing cells.

7. Click OK, and then click Close.

To display an existing scenario in Excel, follow these steps:

1. Click Tools ➤ Scenarios.

2. In the Scenarios list, click the scenario that you want to display.

3. Click Show.

Scenario Example

Given the sample data in Figure A-6, create two scenarios displaying cubic area for a specified length, width, and height, and switch between these scenarios.

1. Click Tools ➤ Scenarios.

2. Click Add.

3. Click the Scenario Name box, and then type **Cube**.

4. Click the Changing Cells box, and then select cells B1 through B3.

5. Click OK.

6. Type **4** in each of the three boxes.

7. Click OK.

8. Click Add.

	A	B	C
1	Length	2	
2	Height	3	
3	Width	5	
4	Cubic Area	30	← B1*B2*B3

Figure A-6. *Scenario sample data*

9. Click the Scenario Name box, and then type **Rectangular Box**.

10. Click OK.

11. Type **5** in the first box, **8** in the second box, and **7** in the third box.

12. Click OK.

13. In the Scenarios list, click Cube, and then click Show. Watch the values change in cells B1 through B4.

14. In the Scenarios list, click Rectangular Box, and then click Show. Watch the values change again in cells B1 through B4.

15. Click Close.

Using Solver

You can use Solver to help find an optimal solution to a problem, based on an exact specified outcome, the lowest possible outcome, or the highest possible outcome. Solver does this by changing the worksheet cell values you specify to produce the selected cell formula's desired value. You can also apply restrictions to the cell values that Solver can use to find the desired value.

Solver Procedure

To create and solve a Solver problem in Excel, follow these steps:

1. Click Tools ➤ Solver.

Note If the Solver command is not available, you must load Solver, and then click Tools ➤ Solver again. To load Solver, click Tools ➤ Add-Ins, select the Solver Add-In check box, and click OK. If the Solver Add-In check box is not available, consult Excel Help to determine how to install Solver (the installation instructions may vary based on your Excel version).

---

2. In the Set Target Cell box, type or click a cell reference for the target cell. The target cell must contain a formula.

3. Do one of the following:

   • To have the value of the target cell be as large as possible, click Max.

   • To have the value of the target cell be as small as possible, click Min.

   • To have the target cell be a certain value, click Value Of, and then type that value in the box.

4. In the By Changing Cells box, type or click a cell reference for the adjustable cells. The adjustable cells must be related directly or indirectly to the target cell.

Tip If you want to have Solver automatically suggest the adjustable cells based on the target cell, click Guess.

---

5. To add any constraints that you want to apply, follow this procedure:

   a. Click Add.

   b. Click the Cell Reference box, and then type or click a cell reference for which you want to constrain the value.

   c. In the operator list, click the relationship (<=, =, >=, Int, or Bin) that you want between the referenced cell and the constraint.

   d. Click the Constraint box, and then type a number, a cell reference, or a formula.

   e. Do one of the following:

      • To accept the constraint and add another, click Add.

      • To accept the constraint and return to the Solver Parameters dialog box, click OK.

6. Click Solve and do one of the following:

   • To keep the solution values on the worksheet, click Keep Solver Solution.

   • To restore the original data on the worksheet, click Restore Original Values.

7. Click OK.

Solver Example

Given the sample data in Figure A-7, use Solver to determine how close you can get to 40 degrees Celsius without exceeding 101 degrees Fahrenheit and without typing over the formula in cell B2.

	A	B	C
1	Degrees Kelvin	300.0	
2	Degrees Fahrenheit	80.3	← CONVERT(B1, "K", "F")
3	Degrees Celsius	26.9	← CONVERT(B2, "F", "C")

Figure A-7. *Solver sample with starting data*

1. Click Tools ➤ Solver.

2. Click Set Target Cell, and then click cell B3.

3. Click Value Of, and then type **40** in the Value Of box.

4. Click Guess.

5. Click Add.

6. Click the Cell Reference Box, and then click cell B2.

7. Click the Constraint box, and then type **101**.

8. Click OK.

9. Click Solve. Compare your results to Figure A-8.

	A	B	C
1	Degrees Kelvin	311.5	
2	Degrees Fahrenheit	101.0	← CONVERT(B1, "K", "F")
3	Degrees Celsius	38.3	← CONVERT(B2, "F", "C")

Figure A-8. *Completed Solver sample*

APPENDIX B

■ ■ ■

Summary of Other Helpful Excel Data Analysis Tools

This appendix briefly summarizes common Excel data analysis tools. These tools are helpful for performing the following tasks:

- Subtotaling and outlining data
- Consolidating data
- Sorting data
- Filtering data
- Conditional cell formatting
- Analyzing online analytical processing (OLAP) data
- Working with PivotTables and PivotCharts

Subtotaling and Outlining Data

Excel can automatically calculate subtotal and grand total lists of cell values. Excel can also outline lists so that you can display or hide the subtotals' detail rows. For example, given a list of geographical regions (such as North, South, East, and West), each of the United States states organized by geographical region, and their total populations, you could display a population subtotal for each geographical region.

To subtotal lists of cell values, follow these steps:

1. Make sure that each column of cell values has a label in the first row and contains similar data, and there are no blank rows or columns within the cell values.

2. Click a cell in the column to subtotal.

3. Optionally, on the Standard toolbar, click Sort Ascending or Sort Descending to group similar rows' cell values together.

4. Click Data ➤ Subtotals. Follow the Subtotal dialog box's directions.

5. Click OK.

6. Optionally, to display or hide subtotal detail rows in subtotaled data, click the outlining buttons numbered 1, 2, and 3 to the side of the subtotaled data, or click the plus or minus symbols under the outlining buttons.

Consolidating Data

Excel can combine the values of several independent groups of cells into a single group, a technique known as *consolidating data*. For example, given four worksheets of yearly sales data from geographical regions (such as North, South, East, and West), you could consolidate this sales data into a single region-wide sales total worksheet for each of the geographical regions for all four years' worth of sales combined, for easier and faster data analysis.

Three common data consolidation techniques are available:

- *Using 3-D references in formulas*: 3-D references are references to cells that span two or more worksheets in a workbook. You can consolidate data using 3-D references in formulas for any type or arrangement of data (this is the preferred data-consolidation technique).

- *By position*: You can consolidate data by position if your data is in the same cell in several cell groups.

- *By category*: You can consolidate data by category if you have data in cell groups that each contain the same row or column labels.

Consolidating Using 3-D References in Formulas

To consolidate data using 3-D references in formulas, follow these steps:

1. On the consolidation worksheet, copy or enter the column labels you want for the consolidated data.

2. Click the cell that you want to contain the consolidated data.

■**Caution** To avoid circular references, make sure that the consolidated sheet is not within the group of sheets specified in the consolidation formula.

---

3. Type a formula in the cell that includes references to the source cells on each worksheet that contains the data you want to consolidate. For example, to combine the data in cell A2 from worksheets Sheet1 through Sheet4 inclusive, you could type =SUM(Sheet1:Sheet4!A2). If the data to consolidate is in different cells on different worksheets, enter a formula such as =SUM(Sheet1!A2,Sheet4!B6).

■**Tip** To enter a reference to one or more cells on the same worksheet (such as Sheet2!C1:C3) in a formula without typing the reference, type the formula up to the point where you need the reference, such as =SUM(, select cells C1 through C3, and then return to the cell with the =SUM(Sheet2!C1:C3 reference displayed to enter additional cells. Be sure to type a comma between each cell value or group of cell values (for example, =SUM(Sheet2!C1:C3,Sheet1!F8).

Consolidating Data by Position or Category

To consolidate data by position or by category, follow these steps:

1. Set up the data to be consolidated by making sure that each separate cell group's column has a label in the first row and contains similar facts, and there are no blank rows or columns within the list.

2. Make sure each cell group is on its own worksheet. Do not put any of the separate cell groups on the worksheet where you want to put the consolidated cell group.

3. Check for the following similarities in the data:

   • If you're consolidating data by position, make sure that each separate cell group has the same basic layout.

   • If you're consolidating data by category, make sure that each of the separate cell groups' column and row labels have identical spelling and capitalization.

4. Give each cell group a unique defined name. To do so, select each cell group in turn, click Insert ➤ Name ➤ Define, type a unique defined name, click Add, and click OK.

5. Click the upper-left cell of the cell group in which you want the consolidated data to appear.

6. Click Data ➤ Consolidate.

7. In the Function list, select the function that you want Excel to use to consolidate the data.

8. Click the Reference box, click the worksheet tab of the first range to consolidate, type the name you gave the cell group, and then click Add. Repeat this step for each cell group.

9. Optionally, select the Create Links to Source Data check box if you want to update the consolidation cell group automatically whenever data in any of the source cell groups changes.

10. Set the Top Row and Left Column check boxes as follows:

    • If you're consolidating data by position, leave the Top Row and Left Column check boxes cleared.

■Note If you're consolidating data by position, Excel does not copy the row or column labels in the source cell groups to the consolidation cell group. If you want row or column labels for the consolidated cell group, copy them from one of the source cell groups or enter them manually.

    • If you're consolidating data by category, select the Top Row and Left Column check boxes as appropriate to specify whether the row and/or column labels are located in the source cell groups' top rows, left columns, or both. Any labels that do not match up with labels in the other source cell groups result in separate rows or columns in the consolidation cell group.

11. Click OK.

Sorting Data

Excel can sort lists of data in ascending or descending alphabetical order or numerical order. For example, you can sort a list of sales transactions so that the most expensive sale appears first in the list.

Sorting in Ascending or Descending Order

To sort rows of data in ascending order (A to Z, or 0 to 9) or descending order (Z to A, or 9 to 0) using a particular column to determine the sort order, follow these steps:

1. Click a cell in the column by which you would like to sort.

2. On the Standard toolbar, click Sort Ascending or Sort Descending.

Sorting by Multiple Columns

To sort rows of data by two or three columns, follow these steps:

1. Click a cell in one of the rows that you want to sort.

2. Click Data ➤ Sort.

3. In the Sort By and Then By lists, select the columns by which you want to sort.

4. Select any other sort options that you want.

5. Click OK.

To sort rows of data by four columns, follow these steps:

1. Click a cell in one of the rows that you want to sort.

2. Click Data ➤ Sort.

3. In the first Sort By list, select the column of least sorting importance to you.

4. Click OK.

5. Click Data ➤ Sort again.

6. In the Sort By and Then By lists, select the other three columns by which you want to sort, starting with the column of most importance to you.

7. Select any other sort options that you want.

8. Click OK.

Sorting by Months or Weekdays

To sort rows of data by months or weekdays, follow these steps:

1. Click a cell in one of the rows that you want to sort.

2. Click Data ➤ Sort.

3. In the Sort By list, select the column by which you want to sort.

4. Click Options.

5. In the First Key Sort Order list, select the custom sort order that you want.

6. Click OK.

7. Select any other sort options that you want.

8. Click OK.

Sorting in Custom Order

To sort rows of data by your own custom sort order, follow these steps:

1. In a group of cells, type the values by which you want to sort, in the order in which you want them, from top to bottom. For example, type the following in a column:

   East

   North

   South

   West

2. Select the group of cells that you just typed.

3. Click Tools ➤ Options, and then click the Custom Lists tab.

4. Click Import, and then click OK.

5. Select a cell in one of the rows that you want to sort.

6. Click Data ➤ Sort.

7. In the Sort By list, select the column by which you want to sort.

8. Click Options.

9. In the First Key Sort Order list, select the custom list that you created. For example, click East, North, South, West.

10. Click OK.

11. Select any other sort options that you want.

12. Click OK.

Sorting by Rows

To sort columns of data by rows, follow these steps:

1. Click a cell in the range you want to sort.

2. Click Data ➤ Sort.

3. Click Options.

4. In the Orientation area, click Sort Left to Right.

5. Click OK.

6. In the Sort By and Then By lists, select the rows by which you want to sort.

7. Select any other sort options that you want.

8. Click OK.

Filtering Data

Excel can restrict a worksheet list to show only cell values that meet specified criteria. For example, you could use the AutoFilter feature to filter a list of rows of manufacturing data so that only daily factory production totals from eastern factories are displayed. You could also use the Advanced Filter feature so that only eastern factories producing between a lower and upper limit of average daily limits are displayed.

Tip In Excel 2003, you can create an *interactive list* from existing data. These lists have built-in data-filtering capabilities as well as features such as automatic data totaling, sorting, resizing, charting, and printing. You can also publish and synchronize changes to the data directly with a Microsoft Windows SharePoint site. To change a group of cells into an interactive list, select the cell group, click Data ➤ List ➤ Create List, and follow the on-screen directions.

Filtering Data with the AutoFilter Feature

To filter data using AutoFilter, follow these steps:

1. Click a cell in the group of cells that you want to filter.

2. Click Data ➤ Filter ➤ AutoFilter.

3. Do one of the following:

   - To display rows with only the smallest or largest cell number values, follow these steps:

     a. Click the arrow in the column that contains the numbers, and then click (Top 10. . .).

     b. In the left list, select Top or Bottom.

     c. In the middle list, type a number.

     d. In the right list, select Items or Percent.

     e. Click OK.

- To display rows that contain only specific cell values, follow these steps:

   a. Click the arrow in the column that contains the values, and then click (Custom).

   b. In the left list, select Equals, Does Not Equal, Contains, Does Not Contain, or another comparison option.

   c. In the box on the right, enter the value you want.

Tip If you need to find text values that share some type of common characters, you can use wildcard characters. A question mark (?) represents any single character; for example, *jo?es* finds *jones* and *jokes*. An asterisk (*) represents any number of characters; for example, **west* finds *Northwest* and *Southwest*. A tilde (~) followed by ?, *, or ~ represents a literal question mark, asterisk, or tilde; for example, *Yes~?* finds *Yes?*.

---

   d. To add another filter clause, click And or Or, and repeat the previous step.

   e. Click OK.

- To display rows that contain only blank or nonblank cell values (only if the column you want to filter contains at least one blank cell), click the arrow in the column that contains the values, and then click (Blanks) or (NonBlanks).

Filtering Data with the Advanced Filter Feature

To filter data using Advanced Filter, follow these steps:

1. Insert at least three blank rows above the group of cells that you want to filter. This blank area will serve as the *criteria cell group* or *criteria range*. The criteria range must have column labels. Make sure there is at least one blank row between the criteria range and the group of cells that you want to filter.

2. In the rows below the column labels, type the criteria that you want to use. Figure B-1 shows examples of criteria.

	A	B
1	Population	
2	> 15,000,000	
3		
4	Population	Population
5	> 2,000,000	<10,000,000
6		
7	State	Population
8	CA	35,484,453
9	ID	1,366,332
10	OR	3,559,596
11	WA	6,131,445

Figure B-1. *Advanced filter criteria. In this example, cells A1 and A2 can be used to return the row where the population exceeds 15 million (CA), and cells A4 through B5 can be used to return the rows where the population is between 2 million and 10 million (OR and WA).*

3. Click a cell in the group of cells that you want to filter.

4. Click Data ➤ Filter ➤ Advanced Filter.

5. Click Filter the List In-Place to hide rows that do not match your filter criteria, or click Copy to Another Location to copy rows that match your filter criteria to another area of the worksheet.

6. Click the List Range box, and then type or select the cell reference for the group of cells that you want to filter.

7. Click the Criteria Range box, and then type or select the cell reference for the criteria range, including the criteria range's column labels.

8. If you clicked Copy to Another Location in step 5, in the Copy To box, type or select the upper-left cell where you want to copy the rows that match your filter criteria.

9. Optionally, if you don't want to display rows with the exact same values more than once, select the Unique Records Only box.

10. Click OK.

Using Conditional Cell Formatting

Excel can change cells' display formats, such as shading or font colors, if specified conditions are met. This technique is known as *conditional formatting*. For example, you could shade a cell green if its value is greater than 100, or you could shade a cell red if its value is less than zero.

To apply, change, or remove conditional cell formatting, follow these steps:

1. Select the cells for which you want to add, change, or remove conditional cell formatting.

2. Click Format ➤ Conditional Formatting.

3. Do one of the following:

   - To add a conditional cell format, follow these steps:

     a. Select Cell Value Is or Formula Is, select the comparison phrase, and then type a value; or type a formula that can return the value True, starting with an equal sign (=).

     b. Click Format.

     c. Select the formatting that you want to apply when the cell value meets the condition or the formula returns the value True.

     d. To add another condition, click Add, and then repeat the previous three steps.

   - To change a conditional cell format, click Format for the condition that you want to change, select any options that you want to change, and then click OK.

   - To remove one or more conditional cell formats, click Delete, select the check boxes for the conditions that you want to delete, and then click OK.

4. Click OK.

Working with OLAP Data

Excel can analyze OLAP data. OLAP, which stands for online analytical processing, is a branch of data storage and data analysis that deals with multidimensional data.

Multidimensional data, also known as *hierarchical data*, is data that is stored and analyzed along several different possible categories, such as time or geographical location. OLAP data sources themselves usually refer to underlying data sources containing from tens of thousands to millions or more individual pieces of data. Because these underlying data sources can typically take more memory and disk space to store, view, and analyze than most personal computers, OLAP data sources contain only summarized data organized into multidimensional or hierarchical categories. For example, an underlying data source may contain tens of millions of individual bank transactions for the last 10 years, while a corresponding OLAP data source might contain these bank transactions summarized by the bank's 40 branches in four geographical regions for each of the last 10 years, for a total of only 1,600 individual data values.

For more information about Excel's OLAP data analysis tools, search for the term "OLAP" in Excel Help.

Working with PivotTables and PivotCharts

PivotTables and PivotCharts are Excel features that allow you to see patterns and trends of large amounts of data in a short amount of time. You can take a lot of individual data values and get faster insights about how the data items are related to each other. If you want to look at the same data insights from additional perspectives, you simply rearrange, or pivot, the data in the Pivot-Tables or PivotCharts accordingly, so that additional insights swing into view.

For example, using PivotTables and PivotCharts, you can take thousands of individual sales transactions and present them in a table that provides a graphical, summarized view of those sales by calendar month. You could then quickly transform the summary view into sales by geographical store location for comparison.

■**Tip** For more information about PivotTables and PivotCharts, read my book *A Complete Guide to PivotTables: A Visual Approach* (Berkeley, CA: Apress, 2004).

For detailed steps on creating PivotTables and PivotCharts, see the "Create a PivotTable Report" topic in Excel Help.

APPENDIX C

■ ■ ■

Summary of Common Excel Data Analysis Functions

This appendix briefly summarizes some common Excel data analysis functions for analyzing statistical, mathematical, and financial data.

Statistical Functions

The following are Excel's common statistical functions:

AVERAGE: Returns the average (mean) of the arguments. The arguments must be numbers or names, arrays of cells, or cell references that contain numbers. For example, =AVERAGE(10,2,3) returns 5.

LARGE: Returns the kth largest value in a data set. For example, =LARGE({100,75,120,95}, 2) returns the second largest value (the number 2 in the function represents the second largest value) in the given data set, or 100.

MAX: Returns the largest value in a set of values. For example, =MAX(100,75,120,95) returns 120.

MEDIAN: Returns the median number in the set of given numbers. The median is the number in the middle of a set of numbers; that is, half the numbers have values that are greater than the median, and half have values that are less. For example, =MEDIAN(20,100,10,80,90) returns 80.

MIN: Returns the smallest value in a set of values. For example, =MIN(100,75,120,95) returns 75.

MODE: Returns the most frequently occurring, or repetitive, value in an array or range of data. For example, =MODE(45,60,45,70,65,100,65,45,100) returns 45.

PERCENTILE: Returns the kth percentile of values in a range. You can use this function to establish a threshold of acceptance. For example, you can determine all sales figures that fall above or below a particular percentile. For example, =PERCENTILE({20,40,95,60,100}, 0.3) returns 44 (44 is the thirtieth percentile—0.3, or 30%—for the given list of values).

PERCENTRANK: Returns the rank of a value in a data set as a percentage of the data set. You can use this function to evaluate the relative standing of a value within a data set, such as the standing of a specific sales figure among all sales figures for a sales region. For example, =PERCENTRANK({20,40,95,60,100}, 40) returns 0.25 (40 is in the twenty-fifth percentile—0.25, or 25%—of the given list of values).

QUARTILE: Returns the quartile of a data set. Quartiles often are used to divide data into groups, such as the top 25% of sales figures for a sales region. For example, =QUARTILE({20,40,95,60,100}, 3) returns 95 (the third quartile, or seventy-fifth percentile, of the given list of values—0 for minimum, 1 for twenty-fifth percentile, 2 for fiftieth percentile, 3 for seventy-fifth percentile, and 4 for maximum).

RANK: Returns the rank of a number in a list of numbers. The rank of a number is its size relative to other values in a list. (If you were to sort the list, the rank of the number would be its position in the list.) For example, =RANK(60,Values,1) returns the number 2 (the second number in the list, where Values is a named cell group containing the values 100, 60, 10, 95, and 100; and 1 means to sort the list in ascending order (specify 0 or omit the last argument to sort the list in descending order).

SMALL: Returns the kth smallest value in a data set. For example, =SMALL({100,75,120,95}, 2) returns the second smallest value (the number 2 in the function represents the second smallest value) in the given data set, or 95.

STDEV: Estimates standard deviation based on a sample. For example, =STDEV(20,40,95,60,100) returns around 34.6 (dispersed from the average value of 63). STDEV assumes that the list is not the entire list of values. If this list is indeed the entire list of values and not just a portion, use STDEVP instead.

■**Note** The standard deviation is another measure of how widely values are dispersed from the average value (the mean). Standard deviation is the square root of the variance (described in the next note). For example, given the three sets {0,0,21,21}, {0,7,14,21}, and {9,10,11,12}, each has an average of 10.5. Their standard deviations are 10.5, about 7.8, and about 1.1, respectively. The third set has a much smaller standard deviation than the other two because its values are all close to 10.5. Most business data analysts use standard deviation instead of variance because standard deviation results are simpler to understand and interpret than variance.

STDEVP: Similar to STDEV, calculates standard deviation, but based on the entire population given as arguments. The standard deviation is a measure of how widely values are dispersed from the average value (the mean). For example, =STDEVP(20,40,95,60,100) returns around 30.9 (dispersed from the average value of 63). STDEVP assumes that the list is the entire list of values. If this list is not the entire list of values but just a portion, use STDEV instead.

VAR: Estimates variance based on a sample. For example, =VAR(20,40,95,60,100) returns 1,195. VAR assumes that the list is not the entire list of values. If this list is indeed the entire list of values and not just a portion, use VARP instead.

Note The variance is one measure of how widely values are dispersed from the average value (the mean). Variance is the square of the standard deviation (described in the previous note). For example, given the three sets {0,0,21,21}, {0,7,14,21}, and {9,10,11,12}, each has an average of 10.5. Their variances are 110.25, 61.25, and 1.25, respectively. The third set has a much smaller variance than the other two because its values are all close to 10.5.

VARP: Similar to VARP, estimates variance, but based on the entire population given as arguments. For example, =VARP(20,40,95,60,100) returns 956. VARP assumes that the list is the entire list of values. If this list is not the entire list of values but just a portion, use VAR instead.

Mathematical Functions

The following are Excel's common mathematical functions:

CEILING: Returns the number rounded up, away from zero, to the nearest multiple of significance. This is helpful, for example, when displaying dollar values rounded up to the nearest quarter dollar. For example, =CEILING(5.16, 0.25) returns 5.25, and =CEILING(5.26, 0.25) returns 5.50.

COMBIN: Returns the number of combinations for a given number of items. This is helpful for determining the total possible number of groups for a given number of items. For example, =COMBIN(6,3) returns 20, which is the number of possible three-item groups that can be formed with six items.

FLOOR: Returns the number rounded down, toward zero, to the nearest multiple of significance. This is helpful, for example, when displaying dollar values rounded down to the nearest quarter dollar. For example, =FLOOR(5.16, 0.25) returns 5.00, and =FLOOR(5.26, 0.25) returns 5.25.

INT: Rounds a number down to the nearest integer. For example, =INT(7.3) returns 7, and =INT(-7.3) returns –8.

MOD: Returns the remainder after the number is divided by the divisor. For example, =MOD(16,3) returns 1 (16 divided by 3 equals 5 with 1 as the remainder). Note that the result has the same sign as the divisor.

MROUND: Returns a number rounded to the desired multiple. For example, =MROUND(17,4) returns 16 (as the nearest multiple of 4 nearest 17 is 16), and =MROUND(17,8) also returns 16 (as the nearest multiple of 8 nearest 17 is also 16). Note that MROUND rounds up, away from zero, if the remainder of dividing the number by the multiple is greater than or equal to half of the value of the multiple.

POWER: Returns the result of a number raised to a power. For example, =POWER(5,3) returns 125 (which is 5 cubed, or 5 raised to the third power). Note that this is the same as typing =5^3.

PRODUCT: Multiplies all the numbers given as arguments and returns the product. For example, =PRODUCT(11,10,12) returns 1,320 (which is 11 multiplied by 10, which is then multiplied by 12). Note that this is the same as typing =11*10*12.

QUOTIENT: Returns the integer portion of a division. Use this function when you want to discard the remainder of a division. For example, =QUOTIENT(137.2,5) returns 27 (137.2 divided by 5 is 27.44, with the fractional portion discarded).

ROUND: Rounds a number to a specified number of digits. For example, =ROUND(12.389,2) returns 12.39 (which is 12.389 rounded to 2 digits), and =ROUND(12.389,0) returns 12 (which is 12.389 rounded to the next whole number).

ROUNDDOWN: Rounds a number down, toward zero. For example, =ROUNDDOWN(12.389,2) returns 12.38, and =ROUNDDOWN(12.389,0) returns 12.

ROUNDUP: Rounds a number up, away from zero. For example, =ROUNDUP(12.389,2) returns 12.39, and =ROUNDUP(12.389,0) returns 13.

SQRT: Returns a positive square root. For example, =SQRT(64) returns 8 (which is the square root of 64).

SUM: Adds all the numbers given as arguments and returns the sum. For example, =SUM(11,10,12) returns 33 (which is 11 plus 10 plus 12). Note that this is the same as typing =11+10+12.

SUMIF: Adds the values specified by given criteria. For example, if =SUMIF(Values, "<80"), and Values is a named cell group containing the numbers 60, 20, 70, 10, and 100, the result is 160 (the combined sum of all of the individual numbers that are less than 80).

TRUNC: Truncates a number to an integer by removing the fractional part of the number. For example, =TRUNC(12.389) returns 12, and =TRUNC(12.389,2) returns 12.38 (removes all fractional parts of the number after the second decimal place).

Financial Functions

The following are Excel's common financial functions:

FV: Returns the future value of an investment based on periodic, constant payments and a constant interest rate. For example, =FV(2.5%/12,120,0,100000,0) returns $128,369.15, which is the future value of $100,000 after 10 years (120 months) of accrued interest paid at a 2.5% annual interest rate with interest compounded monthly.

PMT: Calculates the payment for a loan based on constant payments and a constant interest rate. For example, =PMT(6.7%/12,360,575000,0,1) returns $3,689.75, which is the monthly payment for a 30-year (360-month), $575,000 loan at a 6.7% interest rate calculated monthly.

PPMT: Returns the payment on the principal for a given period for an investment based on periodic, constant payments and a constant interest rate. For example, =PPMT(6.7%/12,12,360,575000,0,1) returns $528.56, which is the payment on the principal on the twelfth month of a 30-year (360-month), $575,000 loan at a 6.7% interest rate calculated monthly.

PV: Returns the present value of an investment. The present value is the total amount that a series of future payments is worth now. For example, =PV(6.7%/12,360,3689.75,0,1) returns $575,000, which is the total amount paid on a 30-year (360-month) loan at a 6.7% interest rate calculated monthly with $3,689.75 monthly payments for the life of the loan.

APPENDIX D
■■■
Additional Excel Data Analysis Resources

This appendix provides a list of some additional useful Excel data analysis resources.

Books

The following books cover Excel's data analysis tools:

- Paul Cornell, *A Complete Guide to PivotTables: A Visual Approach* (Berkeley, CA: Apress, 2004)

- Robert P. Trueblood and John N. Lovett, Jr., *Data Mining and Statistical Analysis Using SQL* (Berkeley, CA: Apress, 2001)

- Michael Kofler, *Definitive Guide to Excel VBA, Second Edition* (Berkeley, CA: Apress, 2003), *Chapter 13: Data Analysis in Excel*

Periodicals

The following periodicals provide useful information about Excel data analysis tools:

- *Inside Microsoft Excel* (Rochester, NY: Element K Journals), http://www.elementkjournals.com

- *Working Smarter with Microsoft Excel* (Glen Ellyn, IL: OneOnOne Computer Training), http://www.working-smarter.com

Web Sites

The following web sites offer Excel data analysis information and examples:

- Microsoft Office Online: Excel 2003 Home Page, http://office.microsoft.com/excel

- Contextures Excel Tips and Techniques, http://www.contextures.com/tiptech.html

- Contextures Sample Spreadsheets, http://www.contextures.com/excelfiles.html

- Frontline Systems, Inc. (Solver developer), http://www.solver.com

Newsgroups

The following newsgroups discuss data analysis with Excel:

- Excel Worksheet Functions, `microsoft.public.excel.worksheet.functions`

- Excel Charts, `microsoft.public.excel.charting`

- Excel General Questions, `microsoft.public.excel.misc`

- Excel New Users, `microsoft.public.excel.newusers`

Index

forums.apress.com

JOIN THE APRESS FORUMS AND BE PART OF OUR COMMUNITY. You'll find discussions that cover topics of interest to IT professionals, programmers, and enthusiasts just like you. If you post a query to one of our forums, you can expect that some of the best minds in the business—especially Apress authors, who all write with *The Expert's Voice™*—will chime in to help you. Why not aim to become one of our most valuable participants (MVPs) and win cool stuff? Here's a sampling of what you'll find:

DATABASES
Data drives everything.

Share information, exchange ideas, and discuss any database programming or administration issues.

INTERNET TECHNOLOGIES AND NETWORKING
Try living without plumbing (and eventually IPv6).

Talk about networking topics including protocols, design, administration, wireless, wired, storage, backup, certifications, trends, and new technologies.

JAVA
We've come a long way from the old Oak tree.

Hang out and discuss Java in whatever flavor you choose: J2SE, J2EE, J2ME, Jakarta, and so on.

MAC OS X
All about the Zen of OS X.

OS X is both the present and the future for Mac apps. Make suggestions, offer up ideas, or boast about your new hardware.

OPEN SOURCE
Source code is good; understanding (open) source is better.

Discuss open source technologies and related topics such as PHP, MySQL, Linux, Perl, Apache, Python, and more.

PROGRAMMING/BUSINESS
Unfortunately, it is.

Talk about the Apress line of books that cover software methodology, best practices, and how programmers interact with the "suits."

WEB DEVELOPMENT/DESIGN
Ugly doesn't cut it anymore, and CGI is absurd.

Help is in sight for your site. Find design solutions for your projects and get ideas for building an interactive Web site.

SECURITY
Lots of bad guys out there—the good guys need help.

Discuss computer and network security issues here. Just don't let anyone else know the answers!

TECHNOLOGY IN ACTION
Cool things. Fun things.

It's after hours. It's time to play. Whether you're into LEGO® MINDSTORMS™ or turning an old PC into a DVR, this is where technology turns into fun.

WINDOWS
No defenestration here.

Ask questions about all aspects of Windows programming, get help on Microsoft technologies covered in Apress books, or provide feedback on any Apress Windows book.

HOW TO PARTICIPATE:
Go to the Apress Forums site at **http://forums.apress.com/**.
Click the New User link.